T0381123

FREEDOM
JUSTICE
COMMUNITY

Voluntary, Self-Governing
Jural Assembly Communities
funded with
Community-Created Credit
give us the
Society that Benefits Everyone

John G Root Jr

BALBOA.PRESS
A DIVISION OF HAY HOUSE

Copyright © 2024 John G Root Jr.

All rights reserved. No part of this book may be used or reproduced by any means, graphic, electronic, or mechanical, including photocopying, recording, taping or by any information storage retrieval system without the written permission of the author except in the case of brief quotations embodied in critical articles and reviews.

Balboa Press books may be ordered through booksellers or by contacting:

Balboa Press
A Division of Hay House
1663 Liberty Drive
Bloomington, IN 47403
www.balboapress.com
844-682-1282

Because of the dynamic nature of the Internet, any web addresses or links contained in this book may have changed since publication and may no longer be valid. The views expressed in this work are solely those of the author and do not necessarily reflect the views of the publisher, and the publisher hereby disclaims any responsibility for them.

The author of this book does not dispense medical advice or prescribe the use of any technique as a form of treatment for physical, emotional, or medical problems without the advice of a physician, either directly or indirectly. The intent of the author is only to offer information of a general nature to help you in your quest for emotional and spiritual well-being. In the event you use any of the information in this book for yourself, which is your constitutional right, the author and the publisher assume no responsibility for your actions.

Any people depicted in stock imagery provided by Getty Images are models, and such images are being used for illustrative purposes only.
Certain stock imagery © Getty Images.

Print information available on the last page.

ISBN: 979-8-7652-5290-1 (sc)
ISBN: 979-8-7652-5291-8 (e)

Balboa Press rev. date: 06/11/2024

CONTENTS

CONTENTS

FOREWORD

As a Unity Team colleague with John dedicated to co-creating the world we know in our hearts is possible, I highly encourage anyone to read this book to learn about the why and the how of co-creating consent-based self-governing communities. John provides comprehensive and practical ideas, with some history for context, on how to co-create a universal society for the benefit of all, in which the individual is Free, society is Just, and communities are Collaborative in providing one another everything we need and desire.

The book begins with understanding the fraudulent and corrupt way banking is done for the benefit of bank shareholders, and how it could be done differently for the benefit of We, the People. Instead of the management and use of money as a private enterprise, and based on usury, rendering us debt and wage slaves, money can and ought to be a public utility that can be used to fund what we in our self-governing communities agree is good.

With an understanding of Natural Law, our inherent freedom and sovereignty, how consciousness is prime, and the importance of self-knowledge, we have the power to choose and create our reality, including following what truly motivates us, our transcendent purpose.

With an understanding of the promise of the Declaration of Independence, namely the protection of our unalienable rights and the necessity of governance to derive its just powers from the consent of the governed, we could fulfill this promise. Not by voting, which can disenfranchise up to 49% of the people, but by using a dynamic system of self-governance, of the people, by the people, and for the people, known as Sociocracy, a governance model using consent-based decision-making among equal individuals based on a well-conceived organizational structure, operating system, and decision-making process that is clear, efficient, transparent, responsive, scalable, and doable. This form of self-governance is akin to the Jeffersonian Ward Republic based on Thomas Jefferson's vision of placing most of the functions of governance in the ward, a small subdivision of a county or municipality, consisting of no more people than can all know one another and personally perform the functions of government to and for one another.

Visionary ways to establish justice include Jural Assemblies, a Grand Jury and Petit jury based on Common Law, in which the only law needed is Do No Harm, and Restorative and Distributive Justice.

Practical ways to collaboratively manage our resources based on a true social science of Economics can result in a collaborative community of members who responsibly address and meet our individual and collective needs and desires.

Chapter 5, Creating the New Model, brings all the ideas together - namely free sovereign people using consent-based decision-making and self-governance; issuing the money for what community members agree is good, using a Common Good payment system, local investing, cooperatives, and open book management; and adjudicating and remediating any harm in jural assemblies, – to realize the ideals of Freedom, Justice, and Community, and co-create the world that we know in our hearts is possible.

The Appendix contained on the Just Abundance website and referenced in the EndNotes provides a wealth of supporting information for leisurely reading and additional inspiration.

With the help of editors, particularly John's wife Rose, this book is a culmination of John's life-long ideas to help us comprehend ourselves and our potential, and realize the promise of a universal humanity capable of governing ourselves and manifesting all that is possible, a free, peaceful, healthy, just, collaborative, life-empowering, and regenerative world where we all thrive.

If not now, then when? If not by us, We, the People at large, then by whom? The visionary as well as practical ideas are here. It's time to roll up our sleeves, put into practice the ideas presented, and manifest a universal society that benefits All. The world is as we dream it. Let's co-create the world of our dreams!

Margaret Arndt
Unity Team member and Agent of Conscious Evolution

DEDICATION AND ACKNOWLEDGEMENTS

This book is dedicated to all the do-gooders, hell-raisers, and light-workers who are, as I am, dedicated to accomplishing their transcendent purpose.

I am grateful to the Unity Team and our aim of coming up with the ideas we need to help unify the Freedom Movement, and ideally, WE, the People at large, and demonstrate that when we are genuinely free, we will create a voluntarist society that benefits everyone.

I am especially grateful to Margaret Arndt who is the administrator of our team and who holds us all together. She is ever vigilant in mitigating the consequences of my know-it-all attitude and requires me to be thorough and clear. She also knows where all the commas go. Further, she is an Agent of Conscious Evolution who contributes her visionary ideas. Niki Hannevig deserves special mention because not only does she often understand what I am desiring to say, but she manages to describe it differently, in a surprising and detailed way, so it is clear what it takes to create healthy communities. Darlene Sartore has a life-empowering perspective on language and long life experience in the Freedom Movement all the way back to and before the Montana Freemen. She is a Chaplain and is creating training for interfaith chaplains which greatly benefits us, the Urantia Chaplains Course. Michele Cunningham is an ever present light in the team; she is funny and disarming, seeing the value in each of us and expressing it. Keith Bell is constantly providing supplemental materials and keeps us connected to the political world. Dave Mosier is creating a version of the Jeffersonian Ward Republic, called Rmarketplace, a decentralized closed-loop private membership international commerce plaza, and is a fount of wisdom about the law in general, Common Law, the UCC, and the Ten Commandments. And not least, it is Brad Herrick who inspired the Unity Team and keeps up with our progress as he tests the limits of the legal system's control of our lives. I am helping him write a book about his path to becoming free and exercising the authority the de facto legal system is required to recognize by its own internal logic.

I am grateful to Stephen Zarlenga (*The Lost Science of Money*); Alexander Del Mar (*The History of Money in America from the Earliest Times to the Establishment of the Constitution*); Bernard Lietaer (*The Future of Money*); Ellen Brown (*Web of Debt*); Thomas Greco (*The End of Money and the Future of Civilization*); David Graeber (*Debt: The First 5000 Years*); Joseph Farrell (*Babylon's Banksters*); Michael Shuman (*Put Your Money Where Your Life Is*); and Rudolf Steiner (*The Threefold Social Order*) for their books and inspiration.

My wife, Roseanna Stanley, is the editor who has made this book as good as we can make it.

Many others have contributed to this book! I am grateful to them as well and trust they know who they are!

John G Root Jr, Spring 2024

INTRODUCTION

The World We Know In Our Hearts

This book aims to describe the essentials for creating the society that benefits everyone, the ideal world we can all describe to each other, the utopia we are taught is unrealistic, but which we envision as possible to create.

The two questions that this book aims to answer are:

1. "Why is the society that benefits everyone considered utopian, and therefore out of reach?"

and:

2. "What kind of society would we create if it were entirely up to us - We, the People?"

The answer to the first question: ("Why is the society that benefits everyone considered utopian, and therefore out of reach?") is that we have a false understanding of the forces that are controlling society. The Official Story attributes the circumstances of our lives to human nature and our government. People are considered selfish, greedy, fearful, and irresponsible and must be controlled by our government; and democracy is considered the best form of government. The truth is, as we all know from our lived experience, if we can get the money to do what we desire to do, we can do it, but if we can't get the money, we can't do it. It thus becomes obvious that money is the controlling factor that orients society and directs human endeavor. The primary tool that the sovereign, the lawgiver, uses to create the conditions in which we live is money creation. Unfortunately, we do not know who the sovereign is, what the money is being issued for, and how money issuance orients society and directs our endeavors. We all have a visceral sense that the wealth discrepancy is not justified, that the billionaires have captured the government, and that the government serves primarily their interests, not ours.

The answer to the second question ("What kind of society would we create if it were entirely up to us - We, the People?") is that we would create the society that benefits everyone when We, the People, remember we are sovereign. When we remember we are sovereign, we will issue the money so that money is not the issue. The questions become: What would you like to dedicate your life to accomplishing? How much will it cost to develop your capacities to do that and inspire collaborators to work with you? How much capital will you and your collaborators require? When the answers to those questions are reasonable, you will issue the money you can be responsible for. The book aims to describe the philosophical ideas and the practical reasons why it is reasonable for each of us to issue the money we each need to capitalize each of our capacities.

The premise of the book is that understanding our desire to be free, to live in a just society, and to belong to a community that relies on our freedom -voluntary initiatives- and sense of justice to provide everything that we need and desire, is the society that benefits everyone. The world we know in our hearts will surely manifest as we engage in a process of knowing ourselves and the nature of money.

Chapter One of the book is about **Money.** If we are to issue money to create the society that benefits everyone, we will need to understand that money is an agreement to use a standard to measure value, and a device to facilitate transparent value-for-value trades. Money is a political power, the primary tool of the sovereign. The idea that we can acquire and accumulate enough money so our money can work for us distorts our understanding of our nature as human beings responsible for our social circumstances. When we properly understand the Nature of Money, it will allow us to create a just society, based on equity not equality. To make that clear: We do not accumulate a lot of clocks so we can have more time, and we know that some people are able to use their time much more productively than others.

Chapter Two is about the **Freedom** of the individual. Freedom is based on self-knowledge - knowing what one is interested in, capable of doing, and how one will make the world a better place for oneself, one's family, one's community and society.

Chapter Three is about the social compact and the administration of **Justice** by free, sovereign individuals which will ensure that the people have the social infrastructure they need to thrive.

Chapter Four is about creating the kind of **Community** and economy which a free and sovereign people, living in a just society, will organize to provide for our needs and desires.

Chapter Five concludes the book with suggestions for **Creating the New Model.** It describes a process that will manifest life-empowering communities in which the individuals are free, at liberty, to express the love that wells up from within and use their gifts to create as they see fit.

The book is relatively short and will only take a few hours to read. In the printed book, an underlined word/phrase/number references an entry in that Chapter's Endnotes. In the eBook, the underlined word or phrase is a hyperlink to the referenced Endnote. Each Endnote has the URL listed for the reference. On the Just Abundance website there are Appendixes with additional extensive references and examples of the supporting evidence necessary to give us a better understanding of ourselves, society, and our potential.

As you read, please be aware that cognitive dissonance may arise as you realize the deceptions in the Official Story. The book intends to be a counterforce to the Official Story and to give a basis for us to tell each other another story: Our Story. Sharing Our Story begins the process of manifesting it.

ONE

Money

We begin our understanding of money with the Official Story that obscures the banking fraud. We then give a brief history of money, especially the American experience, in order to help discern how this fraud evolved. Then we look at the nature of Evil and how banking distorts human nature. This will give us a basis to comprehend why we have not realized the promise of the Declaration of Independence - to transfer the sovereignty from the King to We, the People, - and what we can do to revendicate the Republic that the American Revolution was fought to establish. We conclude with a deep dive into the nature of money as the basis for creating the world we know in our hearts.

The Official Story About Banking

The Official Story about money and banking is that the Government prints money, the people deposit their money in the banks for safety and convenience, and they receive interest on their savings. Banks are intermediaries between savers and borrowers. Banks assume the risks of lending and everything that the bankers deem creditworthy is funded. Banks compete with each other for deposits and banks make it possible to make payments locally and all around the world. Because the banking system is so essential to the functioning of the economy, banks are very well regulated, by each State, by the Federal Government (FDIC), and by the Federal Reserve Bank. Internationally, the Bank for International Settlements (BIS), the Central Bankers Bank, regulates the really big banks that have global reach. Charging interest on loans is justified because the lender is foregoing the opportunity to use their money for something else. Banks respond to the business cycle by making it easy to obtain loans when business is expanding and by tightening credit when the expansion slows. The Federal Reserve System keeps inflation under control, helps mitigate recessions, aims for full employment, and is the lender of last resort to maintain the integrity of the banking system and - most importantly - to keep the money creation process out of the hands of politicians, because money is too important to be subject to the whims of Congress.

The only true thing in the Official Story is that banks facilitate payments between us, locally and all around the world, reliably, if not cheaply. Nothing else in the Official Story about banking is true.

Bank Buildings used to be designed like Roman Temples to make it really clear that their authority to rule us comes from the Gods. This is the Federal Reserve Bank of Chicago.

So many authors, economists, bankers, politicians, etc. have penetrated the lies about banking that the Bank of England, the original and most powerful Central Bank, admitted that the banks *create* the money we believe they are lending us as a "deposit" in our bank account.

> *"Whenever a bank makes a loan, it simultaneously creates a matching deposit in the borrower's bank account, thereby creating new money."*

> \- The Bank of England,
> *Money Creation in the Modern Economy*

Banks *issue* all of our money based on our promise to pay and collateral. They call the Promise to Pay (the Promissory Note) the "Loan", and place it on the Asset side of the bank's balance sheet. They place the so-called "deposit" in our bank account on the Liability side of the bank's balance sheet. Assets are owned and Liabilities are owed.

The Bank of England, *Money Creation in the Modern Economy*, says it succinctly:

> *"Bank deposits are simply a record of how much the bank itself owes its customers. So they are a liability of the bank, not an asset that could be lent out."*

The inescapable conclusion from this revelation is that banks recognize our ability to create value, but they deceive us into believing we have to borrow the money we need from them, for their benefit. Banks do not lend their money. **Banks lend us what they owe us.**

If that is true, then the Official Story can't be true, and the Official Story has been deceiving us about something so fundamental to our lives that we must doubt the veracity of the Official Story altogether. If it is true that banks owe us the money that we think they are lending us, then bank loans are a fraud and we have been conned. However, that revelation, when it sinks in, gives us the solution as well.

Elucidating the Banking Fraud

If the insight, *banks lend us what they owe us*, causes cognitive dissonance, it requires further elucidation. Rather than citing authoritative sources, we can use our own observational and reasoning skills to verify this from our own experience of banking. There are many <u>authoritative sources</u> in the End Notes which point to the Appendix published on the JustAbundance.org website. Our observational skills and ability to reason are key to understanding money and how it rules us. Clarification around this helps explain how we really can issue money to create the society that benefits everyone. Let us apply these skills to the money problem.

About Cash and Cash Deposits

Our understanding of money and the Official Story comes from our childhood. Typically when we were growing up, we most likely understood that the coin we got from the tooth fairy, and the cash we got for our birthday or allowance, was money, and money is what we need to buy what we desire. It is likely that when we started to earn money, we were told to save some of it, so we may have gone to the bank with a parent to open a savings account by depositing the cash we received into our account at the bank. If it was before computers, it was probably a passbook savings account and we got a passbook that showed the amount of our deposit. The next time we took our passbook to the bank to make a deposit, we likely saw printed the amount we deposited and a separate entry called interest. When we had saved up enough money to buy what we desired, we brought our passbook to the bank, the teller gave us cash from our savings account, and our passbook showed the amount of our withdrawal, our remaining balance, and the interest we had earned up to that point. When we got our first real job, we likely got our first checking account, because a checking account was more convenient and more secure than cash. If we got paid in cash, we "deposited" the cash. If we needed cash, we "withdrew" the cash. This all reinforces the idea that cash is the official money, and that, with the words written on the cash note: THIS NOTE IS LEGAL TENDER FOR ALL DEBTS, PUBLIC AND PRIVATE, and pictures of dead presidents, the money is issued by the government.

Cash is what we all think of when we think of money, i.e. the coins and notes in our pockets and wallets that we get from the ATM machine. Cash is the familiar measure of value and the means of exchange and store of value. It is the evidence of value, a record of value, not valuable itself because it does not earn interest. Cash is a non-performing Asset of the bank because it does not "earn" the bank interest. When we need to withdraw a large amount of cash, the bank will want to give us a cashier's check (their liability), not cash (their asset).

When we do what we think of as depositing cash in the bank, the bank does not deposit our cash in a *safe deposit* box with our name on it. Instead, the cash belongs to the bank. It goes into the vault belonging to the bank and becomes an asset of the bank. Since we did not donate the cash to the bank and they did not steal it, there is only one thing we could have done and that is to lend it to the bank. We make a **demand loan** to the bank with every deposit, which means they have to pay it back when we demand it. We know this is true because they pay us a little bit of interest on our NOW checking accounts. NOW stands for Negotiated Order of Withdrawal. Do you recall negotiating the terms of withdrawal?

Takeaways:

1. We falsely believe that the government is issuing the money.
2. When we make a "deposit" in a bank, that does not mean putting something that is ours into the bank for safe keeping. It means making a demand loan to the bank. We are lending the bank money, which is why the bank pays us a little bit of interest on "our" money, and the bank is obligated to pay the money back whenever we demand it.

Do Banks Loan Money?

When we lend money, we lend money we have and it remains our asset and the borrower's liability, but we do not have the use of it until it is paid back. Consider that if banks were lending money the way we lend money, they would have to tell us that we can't withdraw our money because they have lent it to someone else.

> *"...rather than banks receiving deposits when households save and then lending them out, bank lending creates deposits."*

> - The Bank of England,
> *Money Creation in the Modern Economy*

In other words, when the bank so-called "lends" money, it creates a so-called "deposit" into our bank account with *an accounting entry* on their balance sheet. The bank does not actually deposit into our bank account money representing real value. The bank does this when we (the "borrower") agree to make the money the bank creates as a "deposit" valuable with our promissory note. This note is our promise to pay the bank money which represents real value we will create with our intelligent labor, plus interest. In effect, our promissory note payments are in exchange for a bank accounting entry!

If the bank made an actual deposit, it likewise would be a demand loan to the "borrower". Instead, a "deposit" by a bank is on the liability side of the bank's balance sheet because it is based on what it owes us. In effect, the bank issues "credit" as an accounting entry into the "borrower's" account, as the bank's liability, (its promise to pay the "borrower" money), in exchange for the "borrower's" promise to pay the bank money.

In other words, the bank "lends" the "borrower" the "money" that the "borrower" creates with its promise to pay. The bank owes the "borrower", but never actually pays the "borrower" which is like lending the promise of a car, but not lending the car itself! (Can you drive the promise of a car?)

The "borrower" is thereby the creditor, and the bank the debtor! Wow, that can't be – but it is.

Takeaway:

1. Banks do not loan money.
2. Instead, banks issue credit as the economy's accepted medium of exchange by deceiving us which turns it into a form of money that can be spent in the marketplace.
3. This is done with a mere accounting entry based on our ability to create the value of the promissory notes we signed and which we were deceived into believing are for loans that must be repaid, with interest!

Our Experience

Our experiences are what lead us to believe the Official Story that we need to borrow money and from banks who "loan" money.

We need money to purchase what we want. To save up for something we want, we put our money into banks for safekeeping. We use the bank, instead of our piggy bank or safe for saving, because we earn interest. Typically, when we begin earning our living, we discover that we need something, such as a car or a house, that we can't save up enough to buy. So we go to the bank to borrow the money, which we will have to pay back. We now have a monthly payment, principal and interest. We often have a car payment or house payment for most of our lives. A mortgage is usually for 30 years. If we look at the amortization schedule, we see that in the first 15 years, we are paying mostly interest. It is only in the last 15 years, we are paying mostly principal. The amount of interest is more than the principal. It is not likely that we questioned the situation. Even if we did, we had no other viable alternative and found ourselves in a situation where we agreed to buy the bank a house with the interest before we fully paid the principal of the "loan". We chose the neighborhood and the size and type of house that we bought based on the monthly payment we could afford.

Takeaway: In our existing system, we have no choice but to sign so-called loan agreements and make so-called loan payments if we desire to purchase big ticket items. Banking is creating our economic reality.

Defaulting on a "Loan"

Debt and interest are combined into a mathematically calculated monthly payment that is due and payable regardless of the real-world circumstances of our lives. In other words, our lives are about making sure that we are able to make our payments to the bank. If we stop making payments to the bank, the bank can repossess the collateral for the "loan". However, if we had borrowed the money from our rich uncle and then couldn't make the payments because of a change in our life's circumstances, our uncle would likely amend the repayment schedule rather than render us homeless and/or carless. If we declare bankruptcy, we can have the loan from the rich uncle voided, but not the house or car loan from a bank. Although bankruptcy can discharge the loan, we don't get to keep the house or the car because the bank owns the house (it has the deed) or the car (it has the title). We get the deed to the house and the title to the car when the "loan" is paid off.

Since student loans are "unsecured" loans, (i.e. no collateral), the banks had Congress amend the bankruptcy laws in 2005 so that student loans can not be discharged by declaring bankruptcy. This provided a no credit-risk loan for the lender, averaging 7 percent a year. "We've had clients who have tried to get a bankruptcy discharge on federal student loans, but they're unsuccessful the vast majority of the time," says Travis Hornsby, founder of Student Loan Planner. "If your income is above the poverty line and you don't have a permanent disability, your chances are slim."

Takeaway: So-called bank loans are payable regardless of our circumstances, rendering us debt and wage slaves.

Banks Issue the Money In Circulation

Banks issue all of the money in circulation (except coins) as "debt payable to themselves", including the cash one probably believes the Government issues. The Federal Reserve pays the United States Mint to print the Notes, (i.e. the Cash with pictures of dead Presidents on them), that we all think of as money. It pays the cost of printing the notes and then it refunds the seigniorage (the difference between the face value of the notes and their production costs) to the US Treasury. The Federal Reserve only has enough cash printed, to maintain the deception that cash is money issued by the Government. If the Government were issuing the money, why is there a Federal Debt? Is there a need for Congress to borrow the money it needs beyond what it receives in taxes? Also, if only coins are minted debt and interest-free, why doesn't Congress coin enough money to pay off the National Debt? The Constitution says: *"Congress shall have authority to coin money and regulate the value thereof, and of foreign coin and fix the standard of weights and measures"*.

Now the central banks are revealing that banks issue "money" and that they are not merely intermediaries between savers and borrowers. Issuing money is an extraordinary privilege that banks have appropriated to themselves and they want us to believe "it is just how it is" and they are therefore justified in charging interest on so-called "loans" they create with mere accounting entries. Now they want us to believe that Central Bank Digital Currency (CBDC), will give us "better money". CBDC will give the banks total control over where, when, and for what we can spend the money.

Takeaway:

1. The banking system issues all of what we think of as money.

2. Every transaction benefits the privately owned and controlled banks' mandate to serve shareholder profits rather than the broader economy.
3. CBDC will increase the control of the banks over us and the economy.

About Loans

Nearly all the money in circulation that we earn, pay bills with, lend, or invest, was put into circulation by commercial banks making loans. The so-called principal of an interest bearing "loan" circulates until it is "paid back". Everyone with a credit card, a car loan, a mortgage, or other bank loan is paying a monthly amount consisting of principal plus interest to the bank. If we look at what happens in the bank when it receives that payment, we will better understand banking.

The principal part of the "loan" payment reduces the asset of the bank by that amount. The money is conjured with an accounting entry and is removed or extinguished with an accounting entry. The payment against the principal of a "loan" reduces the money supply just as conjuring the principal of a "loan" increases the money supply.

> *Just as taking out a new loan creates money, the repayment of bank loans destroys money....*
>
> *Banks making loans and consumers repaying them are the most significant ways in which bank deposits are created and destroyed in the modern economy. But they are far from the only ways. Deposit creation or destruction will also occur any time the banking sector (including the central bank) buys or sells existing assets from or to consumers, or, more often, from companies or the government."*

- The Bank of England report,
Money Creation in the Modern Economy

The interest part of the loan payment is income to the bank. While some of the interest may be used to pay the expenses of the bank and so circulates as money, the bank is managed to benefit its owners. Every bank loan transfers tribute from the 99% to the 1% systemically, automatically, inexorably.

Since every principal payment extinguishes the money supply, it should be clear that if everyone paid off their bank loans, there would be no money. Even the cash would go to paying off the bank loans. Only coins would be left since they were not issued as debt.

Takeaways:

1. Bank money is conjured with an accounting entry and is removed or extinguished with an accounting entry.
2. The payment against the so-called principal of a loan reduces the money supply just as conjuring the so-called principal of a loan increases the money supply.

The Perpetuation of Loans and the Federal Debt

A bank loan is for principal plus interest. In the case of a typical 30-year mortgage, the interest is more than the principal! The money to pay the interest is never issued, only the principal of the "loan" is conjured into existence. Therefore, the money needed to pay the interest must come from new principal. In order to have a permanent money supply, there must be a principal amount that is never paid down. And it has to be large enough to continually pay the interest on all those bank loans. In the case of the United States, it has to be large enough to support the hegemony of the dollar, the world's reserve currency. Is there a debt that is never paid down and is currently (May '24) over 34 trillion dollars? Take a look at what the national debt is today. It is tracked by the US Debt Clock. Spend some time on that website to see how devastating debt and inflation are to our well-being. By the way, the interest payments on the Federal Debt are probably now the biggest single item in the budget, bigger even than the Military Budget.

Takeaway:

1. Banks do not issue money to pay the interest on so-called loans,
2. There is not enough "money" in the aggregate to pay down all the "loans", resulting in a perpetually increasing national debt.

Compound Interest

There is one other aspect to the Official Story that keeps us believing all is well, and that is the magic of compound interest. The Rule of 72 is a simple formula used to estimate how long it will take for an investment to double in value at a given annual rate of return. For example, at a 1% interest rate compounded annually, it will take 72 (72/1=72) years to double one's money, but at 6%, it will take only 12 years (72/6=12), and at 10%, it will take 7 years and 3 months (72/10=7.2). The prospect of saving or investing enough so that our money can work for us keeps many in the thrall of the existing system. In case that isn't clear, go to the Security and Exchange Commission website and use the calculator they provide to see how quickly one can accumulate enough money so one can join the 1%.

Takeaway: The phenomenon of compound interest makes investing appealing, and renders us captive to the existing system.

Summary

To summarize: Banks create or issue money as interest-bearing debt when we promise to repay the money we believe the bank has, and is lending us. We pay the bank tribute in the form of interest. In other words, we provide the value and the bank conjures the money with an accounting entry as a "deposit" in our so-called loan account at the bank. Now the top priority in our lives is making payments to the bank!

The Official Story about banking is so ingrained and so evil that it takes a while to wrap one's mind around it. The vast majority of bankers believe the Official Story they were trained in. To be clear, we are not impugning bankers and banks. However, we are pointing out the consequences of the Official Story that is maintained by the owners of the Wall Street banks and the Federal Reserve System.

Why is banking evil? The banking cartel has appropriated human nature for the benefit of the powers-that-ought-not-to-be who control the banks.

How did this come about? How did the banking system become the sovereign that issues the money we need to live?

A Condensed History of Money

The Official Story is that civilization arises as a result of surplus agriculture and money was invented as an easy way to barter. This is backwards. As David Graeber points out in his book, *Debt the First 5000 Years*, there is no anthropological evidence that there ever was barter. The distinction between indigenous or tribal societies and what we call civilization is that in tribal societies there is no money. Their economy is based on their relationships, reciprocal relationships, in their clan and tribes, similar to our extended families in previous centuries. What we call civilization is distinguished by the introduction of Money. Money makes it possible to trade (buy and sell) and to have debt with usury, without having a tribal or family type relationship. Accounting, the cities and their markets, and especially debts, etc. only become possible when money is introduced. The more accurate story about the origins of money is that once there is a recognized unit of value, then whatever is needed to fulfill the obligation that results from an agreement (a contract) can be accomplished.

In many early civilizations, the unit of value was an agricultural product, such as a cow or an ox, or a bushel of wheat or barley. Lending and borrowing are the origins of money. A large majority of the clay tablets from the early through late Bronze age in Mesopotamia (Sumer, Babylon) are accounting records of debts, expressed in the then current unit of value, i.e. number of cows or oxen, or in Egypt, in bushels of wheat. Many of these records are of indentured slavery, paying off dowries and debts.

Civilization arose at a time before the separation of the religious and secular powers, when the sovereign was the Priest King who ruled by Divine Right and Providence. When the sovereign established a unit of value as a means of accounting for the value of things, then the infrastructure that characterizes civilization could arise. Food was provided to everyone by people who worked in agriculture. And what they, and the rest of the society, needed was provided by the people whose job it was to meet those needs, such as a wheelwright or a miller. Money made it possible to trade with people outside of the tribe, with whom one did not have a reciprocal relationship. Money made value-for-value trades possible and made the division of labor possible.

Because the unit of value established by the sovereign is only valid in the jurisdiction of the sovereign, international trade and empire-building were accomplished with gold and silver, which have intrinsic value recognized in just about every civilization. This is where the confusion about money arises. If the money is gold or silver, it has intrinsic value and is subject to market forces and is therefore not a reliable measure of value. If the unit of value is established by the lawgiver, the sovereign, then it can serve as a reliable unit of value - in value-for-value trades - that benefit both parties.

In Babylon (late Bronze Age, early Iron Age 2350 to 300 BCE), there is a tremendously significant development that is only recently coming to light about the Babylonian Rhadenites. The Rhadenites may have been the originators of the interest-bearing debt system of money, based on the perceived value of gold and silver, which they controlled. It is possible to trace their efforts to control civilization with debt and usury all the way from Babylon to today. The connection between law and money may have begun with the <u>Code of Hammurabi</u> (1772 BCE), the earliest legal code known to us, that sanctions debts, interest (usury), and slavery as a way to pay a debt. In other words, labor (slave labor) creates value, money measures the value, and society is usually made up of the few lenders who appropriate the value created by the many borrowers.

The Rhadanites were not always successful with their debt and usury control mechanisms. In Ancient Egypt, the understanding of money as a receipt for a good or service that can circulate became established. The Pharaoh (the religious and secular Sovereign) issued the receipts and regulated their value. For example, the Shekel (a receipt for a bushel of wheat delivered to the Pharaoh's warehouse), declined in value over the course of a year by about 10% to account for the loss of value due to warehousing, rodents, spoilage, etc. With each new harvest, the old Shekels were turned in for new Shekels representing the value of the harvest. Because the Shekel depreciated in value over the course of a year, it was not conducive for hoarding and therefore could not be used to accumulate wealth. Egypt's wealth was in the monuments we visit today, demonstrating that when money is not valuable in itself, we naturally invest in things of lasting value.

The Pharaoh could not pay his army with Shekels since their utility was not recognized in the lands his army was conquering. What was universally recognized as having value was money that was valuable in itself, such as gold (or silver). Therefore, receipts for wheat were the money of peace, and gold was the money of war and empire.

Gold and silver are also the money of international trade (between sovereign countries). It is the trading and banking elite that depend on the money being valuable in itself, like gold or silver. The Babylonian Rhadenites populated the trade route between China in the east and Europe in the west. Their wealth was most likely based on exploiting the difference in the gold-silver ratio between the West and the East.

The ratio is expressed by how much silver is needed to buy gold, e.g., 13.5 oz of silver to buy 1 oz of gold. In the West (Babylon, Egypt, Rome, and Byzantium), it was high, between 9 and 16 oz Silver for 1 oz Gold, but in the East (India and Asia), it was 6 or 7 to 1. For commercial leverage and power, one could bring the silver to Asia and buy twice as much gold as one could in Babylon or Rome and then bring the gold back to Babylon or Rome, lend half, and buy silver with the other half and do it again. This history is well hidden, but Del Mar and Zarlenga uncover much of the original documentation of the Gold Silver Ratio as a source of hidden power.

The history of debt is described authoritatively in the book: *Debt, the First 5000 Years*. Below is Amazon's book review:

> "...anthropologist David Graeber presents a stunning reversal of conventional wisdom: he shows that before there was money, there was debt. For more than 5,000 years, since the beginnings of the first agrarian empires, humans have used elaborate credit systems to buy and sell goods, long before the invention of coins or cash. It is in this era, Graeber argues, that we also first encounter a society divided into debtors and creditors.

> Graeber shows that arguments about debt and debt forgiveness have been at the center of political debates from Italy to China, as well as sparking innumerable insurrections. He also brilliantly demonstrates that the language of the ancient works of law and religion (words like "guilt," "sin," and "redemption") derive in large part from ancient debates about debt, and shape even our most basic ideas of right and wrong. We are still fighting these battles today without knowing it."

Greece and Rome

In the Greek and Roman Republics, the Senate issued the money and regulated its value as coins made of iron dipped in vinegar, therefore rendering the coins useless as a metal, (i.e. not valuable in itself). This plentiful money gave rise to the amazingly rich cultures of the Greek and Roman Republics.

When Alexander created the Greek Empire and Caesar Augustus the Roman Empire, Gold, the money of conquest, became the sovereign money. In the Roman Empire, gold was claimed to be backing the currency, and the monetary system became interest-bearing debt.

The Official Story about the fall of the Roman Empire ignores or hides the role of the Roman Emperor as the issuer of the sovereign currency of the Empire. When the Roman Empire collapsed because people increasingly doubted the value and honesty of the Roman currency, (i.e. the same wealth discrepancy problem we are familiar with today), the Dark Ages began. Without the money of the Roman Empire, Feudalism (clergy, nobility, serfs, and only gold and silver as money) set in. Money was scarce because gold and silver was hoarded by the Nobility and the Church and <u>usury</u> was banned, so there was no incentive for debt money.

Middle Ages

The Middle Ages, with its high culture, developed because of Market Money and Tallysticks. Both Market Money and Tally Sticks were currencies that only measured the value of, and facilitated the exchange of, the actual goods and services. For example, Market Money was issued by the market to the vendors or by the vendors themselves, to represent the value of what they brought to the market. As a result, there was no shortage of money in the market and everything for which there was a demand could be exchanged. As a result, the society was prosperous and the culture flourished, giving rise to the Renaissance.

In the cities where the Cathedrals were built, the craft guilds developed and everyone, from the peasant farmers and craftsmen to the religious orders of monks, nuns, and the priests, to the knights and nobility, all enjoyed plenty of leisure time and community celebrations because of all the religious holidays. Usury was banned with odious punishments. One of the features of a currency that only measures value is that it is not hoarded, meaning, it is not considered wealth itself. Money as a measure is only *measuring* value and not *creating* it. The wealth was in the Cathedrals, the churches, the castles, the roads and bridges, the workshops, the towns with their magnificent houses, all of which were so well built we can still visit and admire them today. Interestingly, there was enough gold money for foreign trade.

Bernard Lietaer wrote a book: *The Future of Money, Creating New Wealth, Work And A Wiser World,* about the need for alternative currencies that are generative and not extractive. He also gave an interview in Yes Magazine reproduced on the JustAbundance website in which he says: "Recent studies have revealed that the quality of life for the common laborer in Europe was the highest in the 12th to 13th centuries; perhaps even higher than today. When you can't keep savings in the form of money, you invest them in something that will produce value in the future. So this form of money created an extraordinary boom." Paul Grignon has made an excellent short video called "The Essence of Money, A Medieval Tale" about Market Money. It is well worth watching to grasp the essence of money.

Age of Discovery

Goldsmiths became Bankers, who funded the Age of Discovery. Zarlenga describes how the successors to or the continuation of the Babylonian Rhadenite debt mongers reasserted their control of society by creating the <u>Protestant Reformation</u>. They had the Bible translated into all the common languages. Taking advantage of the new printing technology, pioneered by the Gutenberg Bible, they distributed copies of the Bible widely. Being able to read the Bible in one's native language undermined the monopoly the Catholic Church had on the "Word of God". By identifying and funding the rebellious priests such as Martin Luther and John Calvin, whose interpretation of the Bible led to the protestant work ethic and capitalism, the ban on interest bearing debt was gradually removed, and usury became defined as excessive interest.

The <u>Doctrine of Discovery</u> issued by the Pope in 1493, proclaimed the right of Christian rulers to claim as their possession the lands their explorers discovered and to "save the souls" of all the native peoples who would not convert to Catholicism by enslaving or killing them. The Doctrine was about plundering the New World and Africa for gold. The influx of gold meant that the services of Goldsmiths were in high demand.

Everything that happened subsequently can be understood when we realize that a receipt for gold deposited with a goldsmith for safekeeping was better money than gold. A written receipt was much easier to transport, it was made out to a specific person so was very difficult to spend if stolen, and it was for a specific weight and purity of gold and could be redeemed for gold at any time. The goldsmiths became bankers when they lent receipts for gold which exceeded the amount of gold in their vaults. When people became suspicious that the goldsmiths may not have enough gold to redeem the receipts, there was a run on the bank. The goldsmiths who became bankers obviously belonged to a secret society because they would supply each other with gold when there was a run on any one of their banks. This saved the deception that a receipt for gold can be redeemed for gold. The most important thing for the Banker's secret society to spend their ill gotten wealth on was creating a culture in which people do not understand the banking fraud. They have been amazingly successful!

Colonial America

The thirteen colonies were established by Land Grants and Corporate Charters by the King of England (after defeating the French). The Colonists believed they were Englishmen protected by the Magna Carta and Common Law, and they were loyal to the King. The Governors were appointees of the King and the legislatures were from the white, male, protestant landowners (the American sovereigns or nobility).

The King decreed that the colonists use only English gold coins, but there were never enough English coins to conduct commerce. The English merchants paid for cotton, tobacco, pelts, or cod, with English coins, and the colonists sent the coins right back to England to buy the finished goods they needed, such as pewter, glass, and other manufactured goods.

The problem of scarce money in the Colonies led to many experiments. The New England Woodland Tribes, especially the Iroquois, had a gift economy and no money. They would acknowledge significant gifts and events (births and deaths, and agreements and treaties) with wampum: beads made from shells from the quahog clam, which are mostly white with some purple at the edges. The white beads symbolized Light and Happiness and the purple beads signified death and tragedy.

Replica of the Two Row Wampum Treaty with the
Dutch on Manhattan Island in 1613 The Mohawk
agreed to parallel, equal, and peaceful societies

Wampum was also a symbol for the status or esteem of a member of
the tribe. The Natives would honor the gift from a colonist of a horse
or knife, etc. with wampum, but to the colonist it looked like payment.
Because English money was scarce, wampum served as money with
purple beads being 10 times more valuable than white ones. Wampum
became the predominant coin of the New England Colonies and New
York from around 1650 to the early 1700s.

Wampum as Money

When the English set up factories to manufacture wampum, they
flooded the market and inflated the value away. The same thing
happened to some degree with "bills of credit" issued by the colonial

governments to pay for roads and bridges, the mail, etc.. "Bills of credit" had acceptable value because they were accepted in payment of taxes. These circulated as money.

Benjamin Franklin wrote a pamphlet in 1729 that circulated throughout the Colonies called *A Modest Enquiry into the Nature and Necessity of a Paper-Currency*. It was adopted in one form or another by each Colony. Colonial Scrip was issued as money by the legislature, in proper proportion so that the goods and services pass easily from the producer to the consumer. This meant that money was not scarce and there was no artificial impediment to the productivity of the people. The Colonial economy grew to rival England's, probably surpassing it. The Colonies were self providing! Benjamin Franklin said: "*Experience, more prevalent than all the logic in the World, has fully convinced us all, that paper money has been, and is now of the greatest advantages to the country.*"

At the behest of the Lords of Trade in London, the King and Parliament banned Colonial Scrip, and by 1760, as the Colonies complied, a severe recession set in and created the conditions in which the people realized that they were no longer prosperous because of their loyalty to the Crown. As Ben Franklin said: "*The colonies would have gladly borne a little tax on tea had it not been for the woeful effect of banning their money.*" The Official Story is that it was the tax on tea and the Stamp Act, and the skirmish at Lexington and Concord that started the Colonial Rebellion. Alexander del Mar has a different understanding, which explains what Franklin was saying:

> "*Lexington and Concord were trivial acts of resistance which chiefly concerned those who took part in them and which might have been forgiven; but the creation and circulation of bills of credit by revolutionary assemblies in Massachusetts and Philadelphia, were the acts of a whole people and coming as they did upon the heels of the strenuous efforts made by the Crown to suppress paper money in America they constituted the acts of defiance so contemptuous and insulting to the Crown that forgiveness was thereafter impossible ...*

there was but one course for the Crown to pursue and that was to suppress and punish these acts of rebellion .. Thus the Bills of Credit of this era, which ignorance and prejudice have attempted to belittle into the mere instruments of a reckless financial policy were really the standards of the Revolution. They were more than this: they were the Revolution itself!"

Only the Sovereign may issue money. Counterfeiting, assumption of sovereignty, is considered an unforgivable offense; only Regicide is more serious.

Further, Benjamin Franklin stated: *"There seem to be but three ways for a nation to acquire wealth. The first is by war...This is robbery. The second is by commerce, which is generally cheating. The third is by agriculture, the only honest way, wherein man receives a real increase of the seed thrown into the ground, in a kind of continual miracle, wrought by the hand of God in his favor, as a reward for his innocent life and his virtuous industry."* This insight is evidence that honest money is a receipt for grain.

The Continental Congress issued Continentals as the currency of the Colonial Rebellion. The various Colonies made their currencies convertible to or on a par with the Continentals. They were readily accepted and served as evidence that the colonies were united and would be prosperous once again. The Revolution was funded with money issued by the Congress. The Continental was the essence of the Revolution, the inexcusable affront to the Sovereignty of the King.

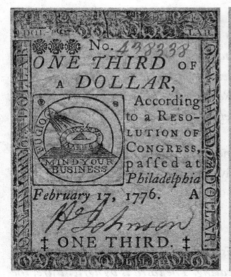 

The <u>British counterfeited the Continental</u> to many times over the authorized issue (probably 8 times). In New York City, which was loyal to the British, the Newspapers carried advertisements for free Continentals, which eventually resulted in the currency inflating and losing most of its value. Since the people did not know that the Continental had been counterfeited, they were persuaded that the problem was that paper money had no intrinsic value. The Constitution stipulates that *Congress shall have the power to coin money and regulate the value thereof and of foreign coin and fix the standard of weights and measures.* To this day, the Treasury issues the coins debt and interest free! How have the banks succeeded in limiting the meaning of coin to not include paper money, or bank credit, or receipt for grain, etc? Why doesn't Congress issue enough large denomination coins to pay off the National Debt?

Hamilton and the Bank of the United States

After the Revolution was won, the Continentals inflated to about 5 cents on the dollar. Hence the phrase "Not worth a Continental" which was used by the banking cartel to disparage Government issued money.

After the Revolution, before the Constitutional Convention, Alexander Hamilton, who later became the Secretary of the Treasury, sent his New York cronies to buy up the Continentals for pennies on the dollar. Then Hamilton persuaded President Washington to redeem the Continentals for face value. This resulted in the fortunes that made up the "Eastern Establishment". Thomas Jefferson strongly objected to the injustice this would represent and said that this would determine the future of the United States. He was certainly right about that.

The First Bank of the United States was proposed by Alexander Hamilton in 1790. It was modeled on the Bank of England and was based on the idea that money is a valuable-in-itself commodity because it is backed by Gold and the money power is too important to be trusted to politicians. The bank was supposed to be capitalized with Gold, but in ways that defy belief, the bank was capitalized with money it issued to the Stockholders, *claiming* to be backed by Gold. The Federal Government received 20% of the stock, but the rest was purchased mostly by the Eastern Establishment and the English and European bankers. The primary tool of the sovereign, issuing the money, was put into the hands of private bankers. The States were prohibited from issuing money by the Constitution. So, the privately owned First Bank of the United States issued the National Currency - the dollar - as a debt payable to itself. This, of course, created the National Debt. The bank had a 20 year charter. Congress was dissatisfied with the performance of the bank and refused to renew its charter. The War of 1812, despite the Official Story, was about punishing the United States for not renewing the British stockholders' private control of the American economy through their bank. Congress got the message and renewed the charter for another 20 years.

Andrew Jackson was the hero of the War of 1812. He knew it was a banker's war and vowed to kill the Bank, which he did. As President, he vetoed the renewal of the bank's charter. His tombstone says "*I killed the bank!*" After surviving three assassination attempts, he paid off the National Debt and had the Federal Government use State Chartered banks. Tragically Andrew Jackson did not understand money well enough to have Congress issue it. Therefore, State Chartered banks issued the national currency supposedly as gold-backed notes, but in reality as loans - debts payable to themselves.

Populism

President Lincoln issued the Greenback as a fiat of the law to fund the Union in the Civil War. The current Official Story is that Greenbacks were an emergency currency not suitable except in war time. However, just like Continentals, which were fiat money and won the Revolution, Congress issued the Greenbacks and Greenbacks won the war.

Populism: The Greenback was so successful that a political movement developed that united the farmers and the factory workers demanding that Greenbacks continue to be issued. This movement went through many iterations of third party politics because then, as now, the banking cartel controlled both major parties. Two quotes from those days:

Peter Cooper in an open letter to President R.B Hayes in 1877:

"This bondage has its manifold center and secret force in more than 2,000 banks that are scattered throughout the country... Such a power of wealth, under the selfish instincts of mankind, will always be able to control the action of our government unless that government is directed by the strict principles of justice and of the public welfare. The bankers will favor a course of special legislation to increase their power ... they will never cease to ask for more ... so long as there is more that can be wrung from the toiling masses of the American People ... The struggle with this money power has been going on from the beginning of the history of this country."

And William Jennings Bryan from his famous <u>Cross of Gold Speech</u>:

"Man is the creature of God and money is the creature of man. Money is made to be the servant of man and I protest against all theories that enthrone money and debase man. The right to coin money and issue money is a function of the government. It is part of sovereignty and can no more be delegated with safety to individuals than we could afford to delegate to private individuals the power to make penal statutes or to levy taxes." and *"If they [the bankers] dare to come out in the open field and defend the gold standard as a good thing, we will fight them to the utmost, having behind us the producing masses of this nation and the world. Supported by the commercial interests, the laboring interests, and the toilers everywhere. We will answer their demand for a gold standard by saying to them: You will not press down upon the brow of labor this crown of thorns, You shall not crucify mankind upon a cross of gold."*

Central Banks

The year 1913 settled the matter and the bankers won. Establishing a central bank had been the goal of the New York Banking Elite and Wall Street since Andrew Jackson "killed the bank". The Central Bank required the Income Tax to pay the interest on the national debt, and the Direct Election of Senators in order to make control of Congress easier with campaign contributions. 1913 was a momentous year in American history since the Bankers got their way. The Income Tax, the Direct Election of Senators, and the Central Bank (called the Federal Reserve System) all happened in 1913. These three reforms subtly, but very powerfully undermined the separation of powers enshrined in the Constitution, and led directly to the expansion of the power of the Federal Government. The income tax and the direct election of Senators both required Constitutional Amendments, because they contravened foundational tenets of the Constitution.

The Income Tax is a direct tax on the people, which was expressly forbidden by the Constitution, and therefore needed the 16th Amendment to be ratified.

> *"The Congress shall have power to lay and collect taxes on incomes, from whatever source derived, without apportionment among the several States, and without regard to any census or enumeration."*

We are expected to comply voluntarily with the tax code by reporting what we owe to the government and paying the entire amount that we owe under the "law". In essence, the tax code requires us to reveal our income to the Federal Government so we can be taxed on our personal productivity.

Pursuant to the IRS, the requirement to pay taxes is not voluntary. The word "voluntary," as used in IRS publications, refers to the system of allowing taxpayers initially to determine the correct amount of tax and complete the appropriate returns, rather than have the government determine tax for them from the outset.

This is <u>Turbo Tax's</u> explanation:

> The U.S. tax code operates on a system of voluntary compliance. Some taxpayers have used the voluntary nature of the tax system to support their claims that they don't have to pay tax at all. However, it isn't the payment of the tax itself that is voluntary. Rather, it's the manner in which people submit their own taxes.....The nature of the voluntary tax system in the U.S. takes the calculation of taxes owed out of the hands of the federal government. You are responsible as an individual taxpayer to calculate what you owe. You're expected to voluntarily comply with the tax code by reporting what you owe to the government and paying the entire amount that you owe under the law.

There are two controversies about the IRS, the first is that there is considerable evidence that numerous states did not ratify the 16th Amendment but were represented as having done so, and the second is that there is no Congressional Legislation establishing the IRS. The IRS harkens back to the 1862 Legislation that the Supreme Court later struck down.

The tax code is a major basis for the social engineering the Congress and the Executive Branch engages in, and the Judicial Branch has given up trying to rectify the consequences. It is also used to punish people who challenge the system.

The Constitution stipulates that the people are represented in the House of Representatives and the States are represented in the Senate. The Legislature of the State, as a sovereign nation, chooses two Senators who will represent their sovereign nation in the Senate. The people of the State have elected their legislators to represent them in their nation State and it is the nation State, not the people, that are represented in the Senate. The people are represented in the House; the States are represented in the Senate. As soon as the direct election of the Senators was implemented, the States were eviscerated, and were no longer represented in Congress. Now the election of Senators is no different than the election of Representatives, and the moneyed interests choose the candidates by the campaigns they fund.

The Federal Reserve was created under false pretenses, so that the banking cartel could get the Central Bank deemed necessary to give them a firmer grip on the American economy and greater profits. In 1907, they created a banking panic and depression. In 1910, after a secret meeting at Jekyll Island, the bankers had Senator Aldrich introduce a bill to create a central bank to regulate the banks, ostensibly to prevent more banking crises. In 1912, Congress convened the Pujo Committee to investigate the Money Trust. They determined that a small group of banks and bankers had an effective monopoly on banking and financing the Industrial Revolution. Aldrich was identified as being in the pocket of the bankers, so his bill was rejected. A new Bill called the Federal Reserve Act was introduced as the nationalization of the Money Trust and was represented as the solution to the findings of the Pujo Commission.

The Federal Reserve Bank - even the name is deceptive, since it is not Federal and it has no reserves. When there were phone books, it was listed after Federal Express, not under the long entry for the Federal Government.

Williams Jenning Bryan was convinced that this returned the sovereignty of money creation to the Congress. The few members of Congress who actually read the bill knew that, as Charles A Limburgh said: "This Federal Reserve Act establishes the most gigantic trust on earth. When the President (Wilson) signs this bill the invisible government of the Monetary Power will be legalized."

Public Banks

The <u>Bank of North Dakota</u> was established in 1919, as the State of North Dakota doing business as the Bank of North Dakota (BND). It has been a real boon to the people of North Dakota. This was a profound initiative by the farmers to create a public bank to benefit the people in the same way that regular banks benefit their owners. However, it never addressed the issue of the banking fraud and usury, and so was not able to initiate real abundance. At the first Public Banking Conference in Philadelphia in 2010 which I attended, it was obvious that the presenter - talking about the BND - believed the Official Story that banks are neutral intermediaries.

The success of the BND has given an impetus to the Public Banking Institute led by Ellen Brown. Her book: *The Web of Debt, the Shocking Truth About Our Money System and How We Can Break Free*, is essential reading to understand how we have become wage and debt slaves. However, to learn the lessons of history, public banks will need to be paired with a call for a Jubilee (debt forgiveness). Usury is the problem. The idea that the money is capable of increasing by virtue of owning it, whether by a private or a public bank perpetuates usury. Equity investments allow the money to measure the increase in value, and require the issuing of new money to represent that increase. Debt-forgiveness and only equity investments (no loans), will heal society, unleash the creativity of the people, and create a just and sustainable abundance.

There is no inherent reason why a Public Bank could not issue money as an equity investment instead of a loan. The stock would be on the asset side, the amount of the investment would be on the liability side of the public bank's balance sheet, and the dividend would be on the Income Statement. I have not seen any proposed legislation that would allow that. Most of the legislation seems to restrict the operation of the Public Bank to accepted banking practices.

American Monetary Institute

Stephen Zarlenga's work is being stewarded and continued at The American Monetary Institute (AMI). As well as the inestimable value of *The Lost Science of Money*, Zarlenga's most significant contribution to monetary reform is the American Monetary Act which would return the issuing power to the Treasury, obviate interest, and fund all the infrastructure the people need to enjoy rising standards of living. Congressman Dennis Kucinich and his Congressional Staff turned the American Monetary Act into the NEEDS Act and introduced it in two successive sessions of Congress. He was redistricted out of Congress for his truth telling. Spending time on the AMI website is well worth it because of the clarity with which the primary sovereign power is represented.

The more recent history is covered under the next section, Evil.

Evil

The role that money and banking play in our lives and the ease with which we accept it, make it very difficult to see the evil behind banks issuing the money we need to live as interest bearing debt payable to themselves. It is profoundly evil because the powers-that-ought-not-to-be have appropriated human nature for their benefit and have used their ill-gotten gains to control us. We, the People, create the value and the banking con transfers a mathematically calculated portion of the wealth we create from us to the banks.

To make this really clear, consider that money facilitates value-for-value trades, and each trade takes place when it will be profitable to both the purchasers and the sellers. The purchaser values the purchase more than the money and so is better off with each purchase, and the sellers set the price so that each exchange will be profitable to them. Transparent, honest exchanges benefit both parties to the exchange and both parties are better off as a result. Exchange creates a surplus. The surplus from exchange is a God-given, inherent in the nature of things, aspect of Human Nature. With all the exchanges that take place daily, weekly, monthly, annually, and over the years, the surplus from exchange is huge. The banks appropriate it with interest because all the money is created as interest bearing debt. It really is diabolical. And, by the way, we know this is true because if the extreme wealth discrepancy were equitably distributed, we would all be way better off. A TIME Magazine article from September 14th 2020, says the elephant in the room is the extreme income inequality resulting from the measures adopted to deal with the pandemic.

"How big is this elephant? A staggering *$50 trillion*. That is how much the upward redistribution of income has cost American workers over the past several decades."

This is not some back-of-the-napkin approximation. According to a groundbreaking new working paper by Carter C. Price and Kathryn Edwards of the RAND Corporation, had the more equitable income distributions of the three decades following World War II (1945 through 1974) merely held steady, the aggregate annual income of Americans earning below the 90th percentile would have been $2.5 trillion higher in the year 2018 alone. That is an amount equal to nearly 12 percent of GDP—enough to more than double median income—enough to pay every single working American in the bottom nine deciles an additional $1,144 a month. Every month. Every single year."

The wealth discrepancy is so extreme that we should find it easy to recognize the extent to which society is controlled by an elite that is not like us.

Of course, it is not just interest that accounts for the wealth discrepancy, it is the power the interest gives the-powers-that-ought-not-to-be to capture the Government, the Media, and the Education, and, in collusion with big tech, enforce the Official Story on the obedient workers who are mostly oblivious to their voluntary servitude.

It isn't banking that is evil - we need a convenient and safe, ubiquitous, and reliable payment system. It is the fraud of conjuring a liability (like fairy dust) and lending it at interest. Elite Bankers had to completely capture the legal system to protect their unconscionable contract. Usury, something for nothing, is the evil. Check out Thomas Aquinas' take on usury, or Aristotles' for that matter. It is the basis for the distortion of our human nature and our confusion about who we are. Interest is evil, an equity stake is not evil. The evil in the equity stake is that stock is perpetual, which is also a lie. The stock needs to expire when what the stock purchase funded is sold, depreciated or expires. Money can always measure the value, it cannot ever be the value.

Our Human Nature

If we appreciate our true nature as divinely inspired men and women, we will see the numerous ways in which human nature is being distorted by the system put in place by the powers-that-ought-not-to-be with their control of the monetary system.

The evil that has scattered the family, that denies the inherent differences between men and women, that has no conscience about using deception, propaganda, compulsion, coercion, deadly force, and war, and that denies our divine inspiration and our capacity to do the good becomes obvious, once one sees it. One does not readily see it because the Banking Cartel, the powers-that-ought-not-to-be, have amassed such a huge percentage of the wealth we all created together, for their purposes, because every bank loan (every mortgage, every car loan, every home equity loan, every credit card, every student loan, etc.) is automatically, systematically, inexorably, transferring our wealth to them. Their vast wealth allows them to own and control all of the Mainstream media, the Education and the textbook companies, etc. so when independent researchers identify them as the source of the evil, we never hear about it in the Official Story. They have designed the culture and society so that the evil seems inevitable, that we have to earn money to live at the expense of following our true purpose, and that it seems to be the inevitable result of an intractable human nature, that we are motivated by fear and greed. We may recognize this because we know that we would never do what the powers-that-ought-not-to-be do. If we question the ready-made concepts from the culture that justify war, etc., and that claim most people are selfish and greedy, and then have conversations with our family, colleagues, and neighbors about how things could and should be, we will find, as the Unity Team did, that we are not unique in our experience and sensibilities. Most everyone experiences the discrepancy between their transcendent purpose and what they do to have money. Most everyone is tempted by the system to compromise their principles.

What we do to earn our living is confusing because when we are spending money to create the life we desire, we feel justified in being egoistic. Each of us spends our money on the things that satisfy our needs and desires. If we had more money, we could create a better life for ourselves. However much money we have, we spend it on the things that will make us better off. This is what we do; it is human nature. When it comes to doing something that we believe in, that serves a transcendent purpose, that benefits others, or our community, we are being altruistic. This is also human nature. We are egoists when we are consuming and altruists when we are producing.

This aspect of human nature is obscured by the system. The system and the culture requires that most of us have to earn money to live. We do that by selling our labor or selling a product or service to get the money we need. If we did not have to earn money, if we all had a right to the capital our capacities warrant, then we would not be confused about the altruistic nature of production. Of course, if what we produce is not valued in the market, it won't be satisfying to produce it. So production is definitely about producing a good or service that people value. Doing something voluntarily for other people that benefits them, that they value, is the definition of altruism. Because we have to use goods and services to earn the money to live, we are conflicted about why we are producing. Generally speaking, the idea that we have to earn our living puts us in a position in which we are conflicted between fulfilling our purpose in life altruistically, and working for pay egotistically. We feel altruistically motivated when we are doing a job to earn money to support our family, but we are often conflicted by some of the requirements of the job that we do not believe in.

Having to earn our living is designed into the structure of our society by the monetary system. It is what we have to do to have the money we need to live. The essence of a true social compact is not that egoism is reliable, rather that altruism is reliable. Competing for the best ideas, or performance, or practices, and collaborating to satisfy our needs and desires, is our true nature. This is obvious if one looks at society as composed of people like ourselves who are motivated to do the good and serve a transcendent purpose, and then also recognize the ready-made concepts from the culture that we are motivated by greed and fear, which keeps us from seeing the obvious!

Do we believe the father of modern economics, Adam Smith, when he points out that everyone pursuing their own self interest will result in the greatest good for the most people? This can only be said and have a ring of truth to it if production is egotistically motivated by the need to earn one's living. Bernard Lietaer has a wonderful take on this in his interview with Sarah van Gelder from Yes! Magazine which one can read on the Just Abundance website. The essence of his message is from Jung's concept of the archetype and its shadows. For example, the Archetype of the King is the honorable leader, courageous and kind, and the shadows are the Weakling and the Tyrant. The Weakling is afraid of being a Tyrant and the Tyrant is afraid of being a Weakling. When we review the history of the past 5,000 years, most of it is about the Tyrant or the Weakling and the suppression of the Goddess, the Great Mother archetype of Abundance. When an archetype is suppressed, the shadows manifest. So when Adam Smith looked at society, he saw the shadows of the Great Mother of Abundance, namely Greed and Fear-of-Scarcity. On the other hand, when an archetype is empowered and celebrated, its essential qualities manifest. If the Mother archetype lives in us, and the society we create together honors the Mother Archetype, we will use a monetary system that creates a Just and Sustainable Abundance.

Bank Loans are one of the main elements that distorts our experience of ourselves in society in that they render us debt and wage slaves. To make this clear, we need to exercise our sense of justice. Human nature is such that we experience our relationships with each other as dependent on our being in integrity with our commitments and reciprocal obligations. When the obligation is about a material thing, we need to know its value in a commonly accepted way - in money as a unit of value. If we borrow the money we need to buy something, we agree how much we owe and the terms of repayment. We are honor bound and justice requires that we make the payments. This is what the powers-that-ought-not-to-be have appropriated. It is our nature to feel obligated to honor the agreements we make about lending and borrowing. A loan is a loan, and is due and payable regardless of what happens in one's life. However if you find out - for example - that the money you borrowed and are repaying with interest was stolen money, and you find out that it was stolen from you by deception, would you still feel obligated to pay it back to the person who stole it? Is that any different from a bank loan? The bank loan creates reality, because the consequences of defaulting on our bank loan are dire. Even when we prove that the loan was made fraudulently, even when the CEO of the bank admits that the money was conjured with an accounting entry, the judges will tell us that they are not permitted to create chaos by ruling the bank loan was fraud and therefore not valid. They may need to be reminded by the lawyer for the bank that judges who rule that bank loans are fraudulent have died shortly after. Ellen Brown described this in her book, *The Web of Debt*, in Chapter Two. "First National Bank of Montgomery vs. Daly" is a case about a bank foreclosure being opposed on the grounds that there was no consideration for the loan.

Loans at interest create reality. Money as equity measures value. This is the key to understanding the inherent evil of interest-bearing bank loans. Rather than measure value, they create reality, and distort our values.

The powers-that-ought-not-to-be, that control the economy with interest-bearing debt and the political system with their ill-gotten gains, use their "charitable" foundations to fund the culture and the "public" educational system. The Official Story taught in schools and reinforced by the Mainstream Media promotes a materialistic survival-of-the-fittest mentality. This hides the real source of economic competition, which is the struggle for the money we need to live. More importantly, it creates obedient workers, mindless drones, and ignorant consumers. It should be called Public Indoctrination, not education. Antony Sutton and John Taylor Gatto talk about this extensively.

Public Education (Public Indoctrination) played a key role in the control by the bankers of the economy because no real understanding of money was ever taught in public schools. Antony Sutton's book about the Yale Skull and Bones Society includes how many of its members manage public education and all the textbooks. John Taylor Gatto documents in detail how university education departments and teacher colleges set the standards for education. What did we learn about the control of the bankers in school?

If usury were banned and obviated, and money only measured value and facilitated value-for-value trades, we would see the evil of usury.

We can see this more realistically if we take a common experience such as we have a good, well-paying job, doing something that we are good at and which does not involve too many compromises. We then feel confident in getting a car loan and buying a house with a 30 year mortgage. Then something happens, such as a pandemic, (2020 - 2022), or a housing bubble burst (2008 - 9), and we get laid off. The only job we can find pays much less, the housing market is in a downturn, we can't sell the house for what we paid for it, and we can't sell the car for a price that lets us fully pay off the bank loans. We will still owe the remaining balances on the bank loans. Now we are doing something other than what we love doing, to make the payments. Most everyone is doing something to ensure they are able to make the payments to the bank. Hopefully, it is something they enjoy doing and are good at. But if not, then people are doing something they'd rather not do in order to pay tribute to the hidden sovereign, the banking cartel.

Housing bubbles and crashes are created by banks with their lending policies; pandemics benefit big pharma; banks and Wall Street have captured the Government and fund the corporatocracy. The way the Banks created the housing bubble and why they burst, it is described on the Just Abundance website in more detail and in the movie The Big Short. This excerpt is from Amazon Prime on the movie.

> The 2008 financial crisis is seen through the eyes of four opportunistic moneymen who foresaw the consequences of the fraudulent mortgage-lending practices of large banks on Wall Street.

The hegemony of the banking cartel is maintained because if one has no moral compass, then Wall Street is the place to make a killing. Even though there are less than 1 in a hundred genuine sociopaths and psychopaths in society, they recruit other sociopaths and psychopaths, and together they make up around 10% of the Wall Street financial "wizards" who maintain the banking fraud. Close to 100% of the Wall Street CEOs are sociopaths, and psychopaths who do not have a sense of conscience or morality. This is increasingly being recognized as a medical aberration, a loss of neurological access to the right brain. It is not a suppressed trait of healthy people. The evils perpetrated by sociopaths and psychopaths should never be used to denigrate human nature altogether. We, the People, have been negligent about recognizing and removing the sociopaths and psychopaths as they have become the leaders in our communities and nation.

Money as interest bearing debt is evil. Does that mean that money is evil? To find out, we will look into the nature of money.

The Nature of Money

Money is an abstract social technology implemented by law, not nature. For money to measure value and serve as a means of exchange, it cannot also be an object of trade, i.e. valuable because we can buy it with an interest payment. Objects of trade are subject to market forces. When money is also an object of trade, it cannot - at the same time - be a reliable measure of value. The banking cartel maintains a propaganda campaign via the social science of economics. One of those distortions is promoting the idea that banks are mere intermediaries between savers and borrowers. In fact, the reverse is true. From the Bank of England Quarterly Bulletin 2014 Q1:

> *"One common misconception is that banks act simply as intermediaries, lending out the deposits that savers place with them."*

To make this clear, suppose we issue enough money to capitalize the capacities of the people to be productive as equity investments in their enterprises. In other words, we do not make a loan but have a stake in the enterprise. Now money can measure the increase or decrease in value without being distorted, and the terms of one's investment can be honored, including an ongoing dividend or losing it all if the expected value is not realized.

Every successful business organizes its employees into a well-coordinated, collaborative unit to accomplish the aim of the business. If the aim of the business is to make a widget of dubious value to provide a profit for the owners, the employees are likely only collaborating because they need the money. If the business is a multi-stakeholder cooperative providing worthwhile products that everyone desires (e.g. healthy food, sustainable products, etc.), and the employee's income is from profit sharing, then the employees will fully enjoy their altruistic motivation and will believe wholeheartedly in what they are doing which provides what is needed and desired in their community.

If all the businesses are multi-stakeholder cooperatives, then they could compete to develop the best business practices which could be adopted by all of them. That is human nature. We aim to learn how to be better at what we do; we desire everyone to acknowledge our accomplishments; and we desire everyone to benefit from our efforts. That is the essence of the society that benefits everyone.

The possibility for creating a society that benefits everyone hinges upon an accurate and comprehensive understanding of money. Understanding the inherent nature of money will allow us to design a monetary system to implement our ideals and goals for our society.

Money measures value. It is a measure, like all the other measures. The Constitution says: *"Congress shall have power ... to coin money and regulate the value thereof and of foreign coin and fix the standard of weights and measures."*

It may seem counterintuitive, but such a simple statement is the essence of the issue. Congress represents the people and the States. It is the People and the States, therefore, that are the sovereign. Money creation is the primary tool the sovereign uses to create the conditions in which the people live. If Congress were to issue the money to pay for the infrastructure, then Congress would be what we believe it should be, the representative of the people and the States. But currently, Congress does not issue the money, therefore Congress is not sovereign. The problem of our government not being the sovereign because it doesn't issue the money has been known throughout American history, but it never becomes part of the Official Story. It is always suppressed. There is a very interesting article in the New York Times from December 6, 1921 about <u>Henry Ford and Thomas Edison</u>, in which Edison explains that the American people, through their Treasury, could issue the money instead of borrowing it, instead of paying the bankers – who contribute nothing to the project – more than twice what the project costs.

Benevolence of Money

The idea that the people can govern themselves and issue money to fund what they agree would be good does not require a plethora of laws. There need be only one law: Do No Harm; and there is only one legitimate function of government: Adjudicate and Remediate Harm.

When everything is a voluntary initiative motivated by love, We, the People, will create what we desire, and remedy any harm by restoring harmony in our community.

This may sound overly idealistic, but when we understand the collaborative nature of the economy in relation to justice in governance and freedom in culture, voluntarism will become the clear way forward.

The surplus from exchange is an aspect of human nature that we are all familiar with but that plays no role in popular culture. Typically we buy and sell things that move through the economy with a price, in a series of exchanges that benefit both parties to the exchange. This is an aspect of human nature that is crucial to understand. The exchange, facilitated by money, is profitable to both parties. The money measures the value, but the decision that what we are buying or selling is more valuable than what we are exchanging it for is based on our determination that we will be better off for the exchange, e.g. it will be profitable to us. With all the exchanges that take place every day, every year, we should all be increasingly better off. We do know that there is a "better off", but it is not benefitting us, rather it is going to the owners of the banks and the multinational monopolies they fund. This problem will be solved when there is a ban on debt and usury (interest) and the ownership of the wealth-generating enterprises is more equitably distributed because the capitalists also labor and the laborers are also capitalists.

When all investments in productive capacity are equity investments that expire when what they funded is sold, depreciated or retired, then money can do a better job of measuring value.

There are three things that we will need to create money, so that it may accurately represent the value.

1. Issue capital as credit, which is the money needed to organize things so that something productive may be created, i.e. the means of production.
2. Increase or decrease the money supply so that there is always the right amount of money in circulation so that the people may purchase everything in demand in the market; and
3. Issue money for consumption, so that the healers, teachers, artists and scientists may buy what they need to produce unmeasurable value, such as governance, science, art, and religion/education.

The money for the means of production that creates material or measurable value must be issued as an equity stake. The increase or decrease in the value of the investment necessitates issuing or removing money from circulation. It is the sense of justice that determines the merit for the distribution of the increase or the decrease. The money for trade (let's call it "trading money") must be increased or decreased to prevent inflation or deflation. This money must be issued or removed in a way that is objective, so that it reflects the productivity in the marketplace and the performance of the overall economy. This can occur through an increase or decrease of a social dividend. The money issued for consumption should always be an equitably distributed dividend to represent the rising standard of living the economy affords. Consumption provides the material basis for the culture that creates unmeasurable value. The dividend will increase and decrease based on the performance of the economy. The dividend obviates the need to determine the value of well-educated, morally guided, voluntarily motivated, divinely inspired people, or for that matter, the severely disabled or ill people requiring continuous care.

What is the value of good governance? Good governance can be described as everyone truthfully saying that the community is as it should be and they are doing their utmost to make it so. Would the tyranny of the majority or the corporate capture of the governance be possible if We, the People, issued the money in the communities where we live? The unmeasurable values should never be paid for, they should be freely given, but the material basis for them needs to be funded. The teacher needs the school, the scientist needs the lab, the artist needs the studio, the clergy needs the church, the Sage needs the stage, etc. Each of those require capital or credit to build.

There is an economic cycle that may be seen clearly with accurate concepts. The cycle begins with an inspiration of someone wanting to do something which transforms nature into a useful good. That inspiration becomes a business plan that requires credit (money) to create the conditions necessary to implement the idea. When the resulting good or service enters the marketplace with a true price - one that does not externalize costs and is not subsidized in some fashion - and there is reasonable demand for it, it will generate enough wealth to make the credit invested valuable as capital. That capital will continue to generate value beyond the value of the credit invested and the enterprise will be ongoingly profitable. The value thus generated by the built infrastructure and all the goods in demand will be the basis for funding all the things that we don't want to have a price, i.e. that are not for sale. Everything that moves through the economy independently of the maker shall have a true price. Everything that is dependent on the person, such as doctors, counselors, and therapists, as well as scientists, artists, educators, and clergy, create unmeasurable value. They should be capitalized so they can do their work by giving them the material basis they need to live. The culture, the science, the art, the morality give the basis for the inspiration. The process is a cycle.

This cycle from inspiration to manifestation to inspiration does not in any way require anything that we usually think of as government. What it does require is an understanding of the flow of values. Inspired and intelligent labor transforming nature into a useful product creates a material value. The product moves from production through distribution to consumption with a price. The highest price is at consumption. Each exchange facilitated by money on the path from production through distribution to consumption is profitable to both parties to the exchange. With all the exchanges that take place every day, week, month, year, etc., it is easy to see that the profit is substantial, especially when loan interest is eliminated. All of the things that consume material values, to create unmeasurable cultural and spiritual values, may be funded with the surplus from exchange.

The costs of the governance infrastructure such as the CourtHouse and and the community center where the people assemble may be paid for from the surplus. However, most of the surplus will go to fund the culture developed by the people who feel called to be the scientists, artists, educators, and clergy receiving the capital their capacities warrant. For example, imagine that in your Ward, or Village, the prevailing education is home schooling and the parents organize common activities for all their children.

This example intends to illustrate the effect of understanding money as the measure of value and not valuable itself, i.e. its nature is to measure value not determine value. Once this sinks in and becomes part of the culture, no one will want the money any more than they want the hours or the inches. We will be grateful that money is a neutral, beneficial force in our society, the same as hours, or inches. In other words, managing our money will be similar to managing our time.

Learning how to regulate the money supply is much like the process that perfected the clock. It took many centuries to develop the clock, and many innovations such as a vibrating quartz crystal were popularized in my lifetime, not to mention the current standard, the atomic clock. We never have to set the clock on our smartphone because the time is being broadcast continuously. We can expect the same level of innovations as we learn how to keep the value of the money constant. However, we do need to come up with a unit of value to use as the constant. It should be something that respects nature and our creativity. It could be an hour of unskilled labor, or a kilowatt of electricity, or a bushel of organic wheat, or something that will still occur to us to use.

Now that we have a reasonably good sense for the primary tool the sovereign uses to create the conditions in which we live, we move on to the individual as sovereign. Sovereign individuals voluntarily working together in complete freedom will create a just and sustainable abundance. So what is necessary to be free is addressed in Chapter Two.

Endnotes

See Just Abundance website for additional information on these topics

- For EndNotes: https://www.justabundance.org/fj
- Appendixes: https://www.justabundance.org/appendixes

Money Creation in the Modern Economy

- The Bank of England (BOE) report, Quarterly Bulletin 2014 Q1: https://www.bankofengland.co.uk/-/media/boe/files/quarterly-bulletin/2014/money-creation-in-the-modern-economy.pdf
- Video: https://www.youtube.com/watch?v=CvRAqR2pAgw

Authoritative Sources To The Banking Fraud

- https://positivemoney.org/2014/03/bank-england-money-money-creation-modern-economy/
- Richard Werner's article, "Can banks individually create money out of nothing? — The theories and the empirical evidence". https://ideas.repec.org/a/eee/finana/v36y2014icp1-19.html
- Alexander Del Mar. https://archive.org/details/historyofmoney in0000alex/page/n3/mode/2up
- Stephen Zarlenga, *The Lost Science of Money.* https://archive.org/details/economics-nat-soc-federal-reserve-stephen-zarlenga-the-lost-science-of-money-the_202309/page/n7/mode/2up
- Bernard Leitar, *The Future of Money.* https://archive.org/details/fe_The_Future_of_Money-Bernard_Lietaer/mode/2up
- Carroll Quigley, *Tragedy & Hope: A History of the World in Our Time* https://www.amazon.com/Tragedy-Hope-History-World-Time/dp/094500110X

Student Loans

The referenced article: https://www.cnbc.com/select/filing-bankruptcy-student-loans/

Student Loan Planner Website

https://www.studentloanplanner.com/

Seigniorage

The difference between the cost of issuing the currency and the face value. The fancy new $100 bills cost 8.6 cents to print. Read what the Fed says: https://www.federalreserve.gov/faqs/currency_12771.htm

US Debt Clock

https://usdebtclock.org

Rule of 72

https://en.wikipedia.org/wiki/Rule_of_72

Security and Exchange Commission website:

https://www.investor.gov/financial-tools-calculators/calculators/compound-interest-calculator

Hammurabi Code

A set of 282 laws which King Hammurabit established. See: The Avalon Project: Code of Hammurabi (https://avalon.law.yale.edu/ancient/hamframe.asp) from the Yale University Library. For example: "117. If any one fail to meet a claim for debt, and sell himself, his wife, his son, and daughter for money or give them away to forced labor: they shall work for three years in the house of the man who bought them, or the proprietor, and in the fourth year they shall be set free."

Surplus Agriculture

For the Official Story read the entry in the encyclopedia on Early Agriculture And The Rise Of Civilization. https://www.encyclopedia.com/science/encyclopedias-almanacs-transcripts-and-maps/early-agriculture-and-rise-civilization

Barter

From Briticanna.com on barter (https://www.britannica.com/money/barter-trade):

Babylonian Rhadenites

- https://www.anumuseum.org.il/blog/radhanites/
- https://www.ancient-origins.net/history-ancient-traditions/radhanites-0013876
- https://en.wikipedia.org/wiki/Radhanite
- https://americans4innovation.blogspot.com/2023/04/the-city-of-london-babylonian-merchant.html

Gold Silver Ratio

There are numerous references to the ways in which the Gold Silver Ratio was exploited in Stephen Zarlenga's book "The Lost Science of Money" for example, from page 85: https://archive.org/details/economics-nat-soc-federal-reserve-stephen-zarlenga-the-lost-science-of-money-the_202309/page/84/mode/2up?q=%22gold+silver+ratio%22

Debt, the First 5000 Years

Amazon's book review: Amazon.com: Debt: The First 5,000 Years, Updated and Expanded eBook: Graeber, David: Kindle Store

Usury

A brief history of usury can be found at the Ayn Rand website. See https://ari.aynrand.org/issues/government-and-business/capitalism/The-Morality-of-Moneylending-A-Short-History/

Bernard Lietaer

The Future of Money, Creating New Wealth, Work And A Wiser World, is out of print. Copies may be found on ebay.

The Essence of Money, A Medieval Tale by Paul Grignon

This video makes it clear that money is not valuable in itself, it is not a commodity, it can be a slip of paper that says the issuer will redeem it for the product they are selling using the customary unit of value, the silver penny. See: The Essence of Money(https://www.youtube.com/watch?v=_dwL9lqVBxY)

Protestant Reformation

- *The Lost Science of Money*, page 237,
- *The Lost Science of Money*, page 256
- *The Lost Science of Money*, page 203

Doctrine of Discovery

- https://www.worldhistory.org/Doctrine_of_Discovery/
- *The Lost Science of Money*, page 210

A Modest Enquiry into the Nature and Necessity of a Paper-Currency

Benjamin Franklin wrote a pamphlet in 1729. See the link for entire document: *https://founders.archives.gov/documents/Franklin/01-01-02-0041*

The Lords of Trade

from *The Lost Science of Money*, page 377

Colonial Scrip

- https://www.michaeljournal.org/articles/social-credit/item/united-states-once-used-their-social-credit
- https://babel.hathitrust.org/cgi/pt?id=uc1.b4420775&seq=34&q1=Colonial+Scrip

Alexander del Mar

The History Of Money In America: From The Earliest Times To The Establishment Of The Constitution (1899), pg 96

https://www.forgottenbooks.com/en/books/TheHistoryof MoneyinAmerica_10620093

The British Counterfeited The Continental

From *The Lost Science of Money.* pages 380-1:

> Counterfeiting was standard British procedure and used as a military weapon. When they earlier fought the Dutch over possession of New Amsterdam (New York) the British had even flooded the colony with Indian wampum, which the Dutch were using for money....

> ...Benjamin Franklin, who had been one of the best printers in America, noted: "The artists they employed performed so well that immense quantities of these counterfeits which issued from the British Government in New York, were circulated among the inhabitants of all the states, before the fraud was detected. This operated significantly in depreciating the whole mass."

President Lincoln Issued The Greenback

- https://archive.schillerinstitute.com/educ/hist/2014/0620-lincoln_financed_war.html
- https://www.thoughtco.com/greenbacks-definition-1773325

Cross of Gold Speech

The most famous speech in American political history was delivered by William Jennings Bryan on July 9, 1896, at the Democratic National Convention in Chicago. The issue was whether to endorse the free coinage of silver at a ratio of silver to gold of 16 to 1. See https://historymatters.gmu.edu/d/5354/

Income Tax

The Sixteenth Amendment, ratified in 1913, expanded on Congress's taxing power. Article I grants Congress authority to collect taxes, but requires direct taxes to be imposed proportional to the population of the states. For further information, see:

- Constitution Annotated: https://constitution.congress.gov/browse/essay/amdt16-1/ALDE_00000260/#ALDF_00001870
- **IRS** (on "voluntary"): https://www.irs.gov/privacy-disclosure/the-truth-about-frivolous-arguments-section-i-a-to-c#voluntary
- **Turbo Tax** website https://turbotax.intuit.com/tax-tips/general/what-does-it-mean-that-taxes-are-voluntary/L5cjhVlhh##

Pujo Committee

In 1912, Chairman of the House Banking and Currency Committee, Arsene P. Pujo convened a special subcommittee to investigate the "money trust". The "money trust" refers to a small group of Wall Street bankers who wielded a powerful control over the nation's finances.

- https://publicintelligence.net/pujo-committee-money-trust-wall-street-banking-cartel-investigation-1912-1913/ and
- https://modernhistoryproject.org/mhp?Article=FedReserve&C=3.0

Bank of North Dakota

(https://bnd.nd.gov/)

The American Monetary Institute (AMI)

https://monetary.org

Biggest Wealth Transfer

- Article in TIME Magazine: "The Top 1% of Americans Have Taken $50 Trillion From the Bottom 90%—And That's Made the U.S. Less Secure" (https://time.com/5888024/50-trillion-income-inequality-america/)
- And the working paper by Price and Edwards, Rand Corporation: https://www.rand.org/pubs/working_papers/WRA516-1.html

Thomas Aquinas

https://oll.libertyfund.org/pages/aquinas-on-usury

Aristotle

- *The Politics*, Book I, Part x, "The Proper Limits of Household Management: The Unnaturalness of Money-lending" Penguin Classics, pg 87
- https://en.wikipedia.org/wiki/Politics_%28Aristotle%29

Media Monopolies

Many articles have been written about the concentration of media ownership.

- Concentration of media ownership - Wikipedia
- media.pdf (harvard.edu)
- How Media Monopolies Are Undermining Democracy and Threatening Net Neutrality | MIT MLK Visiting Scholars & Professors Program
- https://wikis.evergreen.edu/civicintelligence/index.php/Media Monopolies

Education

John Taylor Gatto (December 15, 1935 – October 25, 2018) has written extensively about modern education, criticizing its ideology, history, and consequences. He authored several books. He is best known for his books:

- *Dumbing Us Down: the Hidden Curriculum of Compulsory Schooling,*
- *The Underground History of American Education: A Schoolteacher's Intimate Investigation Into the Problem of Modern Schooling, and*
- *Weapons of Mass Instruction: A Schoolteacher's Journey Through the Dark World of Compulsory Schooling*

First National Bank of Montgomery vs. Daly

Ellen Brown, *The Web of Debt,* in Chapter 2: Behind the Curtain, the Federal Reserve and the Federal Debt. In that Chapter, it is under the subheading: "Taking It to Court"

Skull and Bones

Antony Suton (Feb. 14, 1925 - June 17, 2002) was a British-American writer, researcher, economist, and professor.

- His website: https://antonysutton.com/
- His book, *America's Secret Establishment, An Introduction to the Order of Skull & Bone*s,
- https://www.trineday.com/products/americas-secret-establishment-an-introduction-to-the-order-of-skull-bones#section-info
- From Modern History Project https://modernhistoryproject.org/mhp?Article=SkullBones

John Taylor Gatto

The Underground History of American Education, Volume I: An Intimate Investigation Into the Prison of Modern Schooling. See (https://archive.org/details/TheUndergroundHistoryOfAmericanEducation_758/page/n17/mode/2up)

The Big Short

https://www.amazon.com/Big-Short-Christian-Bale/dp/B0199505OS

Psychopaths and Sociopaths.

- Laura Knight-Jadczyk wrote a book, *Almost Human, A Stunning Look At The Metaphysics Of Evil,* in which she describes the problem of psychopaths and sociopaths who become the financial, political and religious leaders precisely because they have no conscience. Here is the Amazon link: https://www.

amazon.com/Wave-Almost-Human-Stunning-Metaphysics/dp/1897244487

- Additionally, Filley, Christopher M. MD; Kletenik, Isaiah MD; Churchland, Patricia S. PhD published a study in Cognitive and Behavioral Neurology (2020 Dec;33(4):304-307), "Morality and the Brain: The Right Hemisphere and Doing Right". (See https://pubmed.ncbi.nlm.nih.gov/33264160/).

- Their study states that Psychopathy and Sociopathy result from an impaired or missing connection to the right hemisphere of the Brain which is the seat of morality, i.e. a rare abnormality, not an inherent characteristic.

- The following video is a compilation of a series of interviews given by Ronald Bernard, a top Dutch Banker who exposed crimes of the elites, particularly in the banking industry. In this series of interviews, Bernard exposed how elites orchestrated wars, crashed national economies, and used child sacrifices to blackmail its members. https://www.bitchute.com/video/PTV9UqAvYUSp/

Henry Ford and Thomas Edison

The New York Times published an article on December 6, 1921 about Henry Ford's offer to take on a 99-year lease on the unfinished Wilson Hydroelectric Dam for 5 million dollars. In the article, Thomas Edison's quotes are relevant to the money issue. Read the whole article at this link. https://timesmachine.nytimes.com/timesmachine/1921/12/06/98768710.pdf

Social Dividend

https://en.wikipedia.org/wiki/Social_credit

TWO

Freedom

The Declaration of Independence continues to inspire people all over the world: *"All men are created equal and are endowed by their creator with certain unalienable rights, among which are Life, Liberty, and the Pursuit of Happiness."* It is the premise of the Founding Fathers, and of this book, that our rights are unalienable because they are inherent in our nature as human beings. Our creator – however we understand that – has endowed us with the desire to manifest our ideals, to create the circumstances of our life, to be the sovereign. We are sovereign to the extent that we are manifesting the world that we desire, the world we know in our hearts is possible, the world in which the individual is **Free**, society is **Just**, and in our **Communities**, we collaborate to provide each other with everything we need and desire.

This chapter is devoted to the ideas that will give us a profound understanding of Life, Liberty, and the Pursuit of Happiness. Consider that when our life is secure because we have a right to the money our capacities warrant, we will be at Liberty to pursue the one thing that is the true source of happiness and joy, which is the transcendent purpose we dedicate our life to.

Our Freedom, our sovereignty, is a function of our self-knowledge, our understanding of our nature as human beings, the source of our free will.

We will look at why consciousness is prime, i.e. it is creating our reality. We will look at the gap between the perception and the interpretation, and our ability to choose the interpretation. We will debunk the Official Story by looking at child development and education, and discover what truly motivates us. We conclude this chapter with why a heart centered culture depends on the individual being free and self directed in order to pursue Truth, Beauty, and Goodness.

Consciousness As Prime

Realizing the promise of the Declaration of Independence means accessing our inner authority. As a sovereign, we take responsibility for our thoughts, interpretations, and choices. When we no longer unconsciously accept the ready-made preconceptions from the culture, we will be creating the world in which We, the People, are sovereign.

Central to sovereignty is becoming familiar with how our consciousness or awareness is creating the world in which we live.

The Gap

"Between stimulus and response, there is a space. In that space is our power to choose our response. In our response lies our growth and our freedom."

Viktor E. Frankl

The space between stimulus and response may be called "the gap". It is the idea that one needs in order to access one's inner authority, which requires that we "stop, look, and listen", so that we may consciously choose our responses to any stimuli.

The gap is an idea that is both obvious and obscure. It is obvious because we know there is a gap between the sensation or perception that comes to our awareness from our body, senses, memory, etc., and our concepts, interpretations, and responses. It is obscure because the culture automatically gives us ready-made concepts with which to understand just about every stimulus. The Gap is the key to self-knowledge and becoming integrated because we can ask ourselves what response would serve us best or would give us the most agency and joy. The sensation or perception from our body comes to our awareness. It is in our awareness that we can pose the question as to how to interpret that stimulus, sensation, or perception, what concept to use, and what response to make. It may not be immediately obvious, but our lives are a result of the concepts we choose in order to understand our perceptions. The reality in which we live is based on the countless choices we make in response to our perceptions.

Our bodies give us the percept, but our awareness / spirit / heart chooses the concept that gives the percept its meaning.

Observer Effect

There is another aspect of consciousness as prime that bears consideration. When physicists in the early part of the 20th Century began asking the question about what happens at the subatomic level, they discovered that the act of observing what happens changes what happens. This began with the famous experiment in which light is either a wave or a particle depending on the observer. It is called the "observer effect".

> *"I regard consciousness as fundamental. I regard matter as derivative from consciousness. We cannot get behind consciousness. Everything that we talk about, everything that we regard as existing, postulates consciousness."*

Max Planck (the father of quantum physics).

Curiously, the far-reaching implications of this, that we affect what we observe, are never shared in our education or the mainstream media. The Soviets funded their scientists to work with this phenomenon of mind over matter and there is a famous book about it called "Psychic Discoveries Behind the Iron Curtain" by Sheila Ostrander and Lynn Schroeder. The CIA conducted similar research, however it is even less well known. However remote viewing has been well documented and there are online courses to learn it.

Biology of Belief

Consider, for example, the work of Bruce Lipton, when he discovered that the nucleus of the cell and the DNA respond to the stimuli of the cell and produce what the cell calls for. The cell, not the nucleus, determines what genes get expressed. The popular culture would have us believe that we are victims of our genes, but Bruce Lipton's book - which shows this is not true - is called "The Biology of Belief" because our beliefs, not our genes, determine our biology. The observer effect (mind over matter) is determining, i.e. consciousness is creating reality.

Our beliefs, our consciousness, is creating the reality in our bodies and our lives!

Similarly Lissa Rankin, MD, investigated "spontaneous remissions" and documents that the change in consciousness causes the spontaneous remission of, for example, Stage 4 cancer. The biology of belief is on display in all her amazing work. From Amazon's website:

> When *Mind Over Medicine* was first published, it broke new ground in the fertile region where science and spirituality intersect. Through the process of restoring her own health, Dr. Lissa Rankin discovered that the conventional health care she had been taught to practice was missing something crucial: a recognition of the body's innate ability to self-repair and an appreciation for how we can control these self-healing mechanisms with the power of our own consciousness.

> To better understand this phenomenon, she explored peer-reviewed medical literature and found evidence that the medical establishment had been proving that the body can heal itself for over 50 years. She shared her findings and laid out a practical plan for readers to heal themselves in this profoundly wise book—a New York Times bestseller and now a classic guide for people who are on a healing journey from illness, injury, or trauma.

> In the years since then, Dr. Rankin has deepened her exploration of the world's healing tradition and her understanding of the healing power we hold within ourselves—if only we can tap into it. This revised edition of *Mind Over Medicine* reflects her latest research, evolving wisdom, and work with clients and students in her healing community, as well as with doctors and other healers in her Whole Health Medicine Institute.

In her books, TEDx talks and in many of her blog posts, Dr. Rankin talks about how the body is equipped with natural self-repair mechanisms that can be flipped on or off with thoughts, beliefs, and feelings that originate in the mind. This is great news, because it means, in essence, that we can heal ourselves through the power of our own consciousness.

> *"The secret to spontaneous healing may be the one thing our quick fix culture resists - a deep dive into the question 'What will it take to live a life my body will love?'"*

> – Lissa Rankin. MD.
> from *The Mysteries Of Spontaneous Healing*

Lissa Rankin's life and work are another profound example of our ability to create reality.

Consciousness Creating Reality

Jill Bolte Taylor is a brain scientist (neuroanatomist) who experienced a stroke that wiped out the functioning of her left hemisphere. She experienced the right hemisphere of her brain as energy streaming into her through all her senses, connecting her to the universe, in euphoric oneness, with no limits, just pure love. The right side of our brains are all about NOW, this present moment, being connected to the whole universe, and the immediate circumstances of our surroundings. After eight years of her essential self engaging her right brain to heal her left brain, she recovered from not being able to speak, walk, or remember anything of her life. She wrote a book and gave a famous TED talk called My Stroke of Genius, which went viral and introduced the world to TED talks.

She has written a new book: *Whole Brain Living – the Anatomy of Choice and the Four Characters That Drive Our Life*. Here's a brief description about the basic concepts from her website:

For half a century we have been trained to believe that our right brain hemisphere is our emotional brain, while our left brain houses our rational thinking. Now neuroscience shows that it's not that in fact, our emotional limbic tissue is evenly divided between our two hemispheres. Consequently, each hemisphere has both an emotional brain and a thinking brain. In this groundbreaking new book, Dr. Jill Bolte Taylor presents these four distinct modules of cells as four characters that make up who we are: Character 1, Left Thinking; Character 2, Left Emotion; Character 3, Right Emotion; and Character 4, Right Thinking.

Everything we think, feel, or do is dependent upon brain cells to perform that function. Since each of the Four Characters stems from specific groups of cells that feel unique inside of our body, they each display particular skills, feel specific emotions, or think distinctive thoughts. In Whole Brain Living, Dr. Taylor shows us how to get acquainted with our own Four Characters, observe how they show up in our daily life, and learn to identify and relate to them in others as well. And she introduces a practice called the Brain Huddle—a tool for bringing our Four Characters into conversation with one another so we can tap their respective strengths and choose which one to embody in any situation.

The more we become familiar with each of the characters in ourselves and others, the more power we gain over our thoughts, our feelings, our relationships, and our lives. Indeed, we discover that we have the power to choose who and how we want to be in every moment. And when our Four Characters work together and balance one another as a whole brain, we gain a radical new road map to deep inner peace.

As Dr. Taylor says: "We have the power to choose who and how we want to be in the world each and every moment, regardless of what external circumstances we find ourselves in." Her life story is further confirmation that our consciousness is creating our reality.

Thinking with Our Hearts

What does it mean when we say "the world we know in our hearts"? It means that we can learn to think with our hearts. Thinking with our hearts naturally creates a heart centered reality as we recognize the power of our heart-to-heart connections and base our society on our ability to recognize and act out of our love for ourselves, each other, and our community.

The HeartMath Institute's founder, Doc Childre, believes "the intelligence of the human heart is a powerful force that can lead humanity away from the destructive cycles of stress and discord toward a future of lasting peace and harmony". The institute has spent over 33 years in scientific research on the psychophysiology of stress, resilience, and the interactions between the heart and brain. From their website:

> Most of us have been taught in school that the heart is constantly responding to "orders" sent by the brain in the form of neural signals. However, it is not as commonly known that the heart actually sends more signals to the brain than the brain sends to the heart! Moreover, these heart signals have a significant effect on brain function—influencing emotional processing as well as higher cognitive faculties such as attention, perception, memory, and problem-solving. In other words, not only does the heart respond to the brain, but the brain continuously responds to the heart.

> HeartMath research has demonstrated that different patterns of heart activity (which accompany different emotional states) have distinct effects on cognitive and emotional function. During stress and negative emotions, when the heart rhythm pattern

66

is erratic and disordered, the corresponding pattern of neural signals traveling from the heart to the brain inhibits higher cognitive functions. This limits our ability to think clearly, remember, learn, reason, and make effective decisions. (This helps explain why we may often act impulsively and unwisely when we're under stress.) The heart's input to the brain during stressful or negative emotions also has a profound effect on the brain's emotional processes—actually serving to reinforce the emotional experience of stress.

In contrast, the more ordered and stable pattern of the heart's input to the brain during positive emotional states has the opposite effect—it facilitates cognitive function and reinforces positive feelings and emotional stability. This means that learning to generate increased heart rhythm coherence, by sustaining positive emotions, not only benefits the entire body, but also profoundly affects how we perceive, think, feel, and perform.

The HeartMath Institute has an extensive collection of free resources and downloadable materials to learn how to be heart-centered. They offer a variety of programs and tools for expanding our heart connections including practical solutions for our personal growth, health, and life fulfillment.

Joseph Chilton Pearce teaches us that our heart can teach us to think in a new and loving way:

> *"About sixty to sixty-five percent of all the cells in the heart are neural cells which are precisely the same as in the brain, functioning in precisely the same way, monitoring and maintaining control of the entire mind/brain/body physical process as well as direct unmediated connections between the heart and the emotional, cognitive structures of the brain. Secondly, the heart is the major endocrine glandular structure of the body, which Roget found to be*

producing the hormones that profoundly affect the operations of body, brain, and mind. Thirdly, the heart produces two and a half watts of electrical energy at each pulsation, creating an electromagnetic field identical to the electromagnetic field around the earth. The electromagnetic field of the heart surrounds the body from a distance of twelve to twenty-five feet outward and encompasses power waves such as radio and light waves which comprise the principal source of information upon which the body and brain build our neural conception and perception of the world itself."

Another quote from Joseph Chilton Pearce, from the same interview:

"… our whole cosmology will shift dramatically when we realize what I call the 'holographic heart.' But, you see, at the very time we're moving into a period of total chaos and collapse, this other incredible thing is simply gathering. I think of Ilya Prigogine's comments that so long as a system is stable, or at an equilibrium, you can't change it, but as it moves toward disequilibrium and falls into chaos then the slightest bit of coherent energy can bring it into a new structure. What you find in Waldorf families, and people who read Wild Duck Review, and others, may seem small, but they will be the islands of coherent energy which then bring about the organized, entrained energy for a new situation. I think it will happen very rapidly."

I have lived with this idea that we may learn to think with our hearts since I heard about it in an Anthroposophical study group when I was 19. Imagine what the world will be like and how we will manifest Freedom, Justice, and Community, when we are learning together to think with our hearts.

*"And now here is my secret,
a very simple secret:
It is only with the heart
that one can see rightly;*

what is essential is invisible to the eye."

~ Antoine de Saint-Exupéry,
The Little Prince

"The best and most beautiful things in the world cannot be seen or touched, but must be felt with the heart."

~ Helen Keller

For a complimentary description of the power of our consciousness, you may enjoy the *Handbook for the New Paradigm* written by "spirit", published by George Green, and available on their website as a PDF. It is a very detailed and inspiring explanation of how choosing love over fear is what humanity will need to learn before being welcomed into the universal family beyond Earth. Read an excerpt linked in the EndNotes.

The idea that consciousness is prime, or that our consciousness is creating the reality in which we are living, is the key idea to understanding why we will be able to create a society that benefits everyone. Maintaining our awareness of the primacy of our consciousness is very difficult, as we can each attest. It is difficult because we must overcome the hardwiring of the habitual ways of thinking, feeling, and doing we learned in childhood. We may be inspired to work at changing our beliefs when we realize that we will be creating a culture in which the children growing up will eventually have a hardwired understanding of their agency and sovereignty. Perhaps it will take more than one or two generations, but we can begin with confidence knowing that we have the inherent potential to "create heaven on earth", the world that results from being inspired by truth, beauty, and goodness.

The Laws Of Nature And Of Nature's God

The Laws of Nature and of Nature's God is a phrase from the <u>Declaration of Independence</u>. It is a key concept for understanding ourselves and society.

> *"When in the Course of human events, it becomes necessary for one people to dissolve the political bands which have connected them with another, and to assume among the powers of the earth, the separate and equal station to which the **Laws of Nature and of Nature's God** entitle them, a decent respect to the opinions of mankind requires that they should declare the causes which impel them to the separation."*

- Declaration of Independence (emphasis added).

We believe that Thomas Jefferson used "the Laws of Nature and of Nature's God", instead of citing a Christian source, in describing the separate and equal station to which we are entitled, so as to ground our sovereignty in a source that applies to all human beings regardless of their religious views. We, as living, breathing, conscious beings, embody the Laws of Nature and of Nature's God; it is our human nature. Essential to our human nature and the basis of our social life is our ability to reason together. When we are reasoning together, with an awareness of our power to choose the ideas that will serve us the best, we are in our truly human element.

Human Nature

Human nature is about the twin primary motivators of freedom and love, i.e. our desire for autonomy and our desire for community. My life experience tells me that because I am male I tend to value freedom over love, and my wife and the other women in my life seem to value love over freedom.

Society is made up of men and women, who are very different from one another. The male archetype values freedom more than love, and the female archetype values love over freedom. Typically men are hunters, women are gatherers. Men protect and provide, Women nurture and educate. Men are aggressive, Women are receptive. Men are logical. Women are relational. The list of complimentary opposites is long. And each contains the other: women will go to great lengths and make profound sacrifices to protect and/or provide for their family and community, and men will forgo their freedom and gladly submit to a nurturing labor of love. Both men and women express their freedom and their love in the ways in which they take up a task or profession and learn its nature so that they may do right by it and learn to do it increasingly well.

Human nature includes both male and female archetypes and thus involves honoring the opposites and celebrating the differences. One of the best images to express that is Yin and Yang. The image shows the dynamic of the whole. The white and black are opposites, but each contains the other. They fit together dynamically and perfectly. They embody celebrating the differences.

Human beings are motivated by the love that wells up in them and by their desire for freedom. Because love and freedom are connected parts of a whole, it seems that each requires the other. If one is genuinely free, one will be free to express one's love. If one truly loves another person, one will do what is necessary to assure the other's freedom. If one loves a particular task, profession, or role, one will make sure to love it enough so as to learn its inherent nature. What does it mean to be a father, a scientist, an artist, a pastor, a teacher, a philosopher, an entrepreneur, a detective, or a judge, etc.? I need to know the true nature of my role, and I need to love being what I choose to be. If I embody its true nature, I will be perceived as a genuine scientist, artist, teacher, etc. Being free means loving, and loving means being free, i.e. not coerced. A lack of love robs freedom of its value; a lack of freedom denies love.

So that we may better understand the Laws of Nature and of Nature's God, consider the natural order of things. The mother and father receive the child into the family and the child grows up surrounded with loving family members. The family is part of an extended family or a clan. The clan (extended family) is part of a tribe or community and the child grows up in the context of the community, learning the values of their community and being encouraged to understand themselves and choose a life path that will be truly soul satisfying and bring them true joy.

As the family goes, so goes the civilization. This idea is key to understanding how we will create a society that benefits everyone.

There is social science research that shows that people who grow up with their grandparents in their lives, live longer, soul-satisfying lives. It is called the Grandmother effect. "Children who grow up in multigenerational homes have better high school graduation and college enrollment rates and fewer emotional and behavioral problems than those who don't." Are the powers-that-ought-not-to-be creating social conditions in which even the nuclear family, much less the extended family, is unable to fulfill its natural function? Do children grow up in a loving tribe? Or do they grow up in a culture based on fear and in which their parents are stressed out with the need to "earn their living"? Is it possible that women's liberation (funded by the major charitable foundations, including the Rockefeller Fund) had a hidden agenda, namely to increase the debt servitude of the nuclear family, drawing women into the workforce, and denying the children the benefits of a harmonious family life. While not all women desire to be stay-at-home moms, they all desire to give their children the best childhood the culture will afford.

Child Development

Rudolf Steiner, the founder of Waldorf Schools, describes that in the first 7 years, the child learns its body, social skills, and behavioral expectations with no capacity for judging them as good or evil: it's just the way it is, or "good". In the second seven years, until puberty, the child experiences everything as beautiful, learning through play and their imaginations. In the Waldorf Schools, the children learn through art, creativity, and play. They even make their own beautifully illustrated books! At puberty, the child's orientation shifts to discovering the truth. Comprehending the world, learning to think logically, and discerning good and evil becomes of paramount importance. During the period from around age 15 to 21, the part of the brain known as the neocortex or prefrontal lobes develops. These are known as the silent areas of the brain as they are not yet being fully used, or at least only the lower part is.

Joseph Chilton Pearce describes in his books, especially in *Evolution's End: Claiming the Potential of Our Intelligence,* all the neuroanatomy research about the development of the brain; that in each stage of development, what has been learned becomes myelinated or hard-wired, no longer needing consciousness to maintain it. The brain dissolves the unused neural pathways and reconfigures with the new pathways that make the new learning automatic and even fixed. We may observe this directly as we watch the baby discover that it is its own hand that is moving in front of its face. Then after a few days or weeks, that recognition becomes hard-wired, not requiring any consciousness at all. Just think what happens when a child is abused and doesn't have the ability to discern it as abuse: it's just how it is. Their response to abuse becomes hardwired. If our school experiences become hardwired, is it any wonder that we accept the pecking order and the ugliness? If in high school we have no opportunity to explore what is true, how will our ability to discern truth develop?

We have huge potential in our development. Just imagine what we will be capable of when we free ourselves of the limiting beliefs from the culture and learn to use the full extent of the latent capacity of our brains! In his book, *The Biology of Transcendence*, Joseph Chilton Pearce takes it a step further by showing how we are biologically predisposed to become transcendent. The book is about the Heart Brain connection and how our culture keeps us from experiencing our ability to think with our hearts. When we are learning to think with our hearts our biology supports our ability to transcend our limitations and participate in creation

Education

The current educational system is doing untold damage to children who are subject to compulsory schooling. Compulsory schooling is about learning how to accept authority (aka be obedient), how to fit in, and how to be "normal". Most of the subject matter is telling the Official Story, based on materialistic science, lies about our history and politics, and denigration of any of the alternative worldviews that would contribute to our ability to conceive ourselves as creative beings capable of creating a society that benefits everyone. In his books and videos on education, John Taylor Gatto has documented the transformation of education into compulsory schooling and its dire effects on human health and well-being. He is a champion of homeschooling and unschooling because he understands that our children have been stolen from us and schooled to comply with social expectations and values that we, most likely, do not agree with at all.

In the world we will create together, we will all be helping each other to overcome the limiting beliefs from our education and the consequences of our childhood traumas. This is key to understanding our challenges and our potential.

What Truly Motivates Us

A demonstration of what truly motivates us is in Dan Pink's book, *DRIVE: The Surprising Truth about what Motivates Us* and video. The study that led to the "surprise" was originally funded by the Federal Reserve to prove the importance of money motivation. When the research did not reveal what the Federal Reserve paid for, it was suppressed. Dan Pink asserts that the secret to high performance and satisfaction - at work, at school, and at home - is the deeply human need to direct our own lives, to learn and create new things, and to do better by ourselves and our world. He argues that human motivation is largely intrinsic and that the aspects of this motivation can be divided into autonomy, mastery, and purpose. He argues against old models of motivation driven by rewards and fear of punishment, dominated by extrinsic factors such as money.

While Dan Pink's book is a bestseller, why would most of us not have heard about it or learned the significance of its findings? Could it be because it contradicts the Official Story and is therefore ignored? The surprise is that money is not motivating, except if we don't have enough money to accomplish the transcendent purpose we each desire to dedicate our lives to! The research shows that we desire to pursue our transcendent purpose autonomously, the way we see it needs to be done, and we desire to develop our skills so as to pursue our transcendent purpose increasingly well. The implication of this is far reaching, namely if we gave everyone the money they need to live and the capital (money) their capacity to create value warrants, human nature is such that people would work enthusiastically, diligently, collaboratively, and effectively to accomplish what they feel called to do.

> *"The things to do are: the things that need doing: that you see need to be done, and that no one else seems to see need to be done. Then you will conceive your own way of doing that which needs to be done — that no one else has told you to do or how to do it."*
>
> - Buckminster Fuller

> *"Those seeking meaning in work should try to identify and nurture a **transcendent purpose**. By identifying a life goal that extends beyond one's own immediate experience, people could be encouraged*

to think in terms of how their skills uniquely meet the most pressing and important needs of the world."

- Dr Rob Archer

Nature's Laws

Nature and Human Nature is such that everything is in a dynamic relationship with everything else. Everything grows and decays. Everything is born, grows, and dies. It is not just the plants and animals that grow and decay. Even the mountains and rivers grow and decay, just on a longer timeframe. Out of order, comes chaos. And chaos gives way to order. Everything is mutually interdependent.

Our societies are totally dependent on the goods and services that Nature provides (air, water, soil, plants, animals, warmth and light, weather, etc.), and Nature depends on society to respect its needs and limits. The Communities that we will organize will create the life empowering, sustainable abundance that is the natural result of finding the right relationship between our human creativity and the fecundity of nature. Initially, we will be making the necessary sacrifices to learn how to be together. When we have created Communities based on our ability to consent together, we will expect them to shift from requiring our sacrifices to serving our individual goals and desires. The prospect of creating the social conditions in which each one of us is empowered to become our best selves and accomplish our life's mission is the motivation for the initial sacrifices. And, we will cultivate an awareness of the growth and decay cycle of our governance over at least seven generations, so that we may become as wise as is our nature.

The Challenge

What I grasped from what Ilya Prigogine, Bruce Lipton, Lissa Ranking, Jill Taylor, Joseph Pearce, and others have laid out in their books and lives is that there is no hereditary or biological or genetic impediment to our ability to transcend, there is no inherent aspect of our human nature that is limiting us, there are only mistaken beliefs. I assert that these mistaken beliefs are maintained by institutions funded by the sociopaths and psychopaths that are the powers-that-ought-not-to-be controlling the banking system and herding us toward their technocratic, transhumanist, totalitarian dystopia.

The challenge for the human being and for the society in which We, the People, participate in our own governance is to assure that the individuals are free to accomplish whatever motivates them. The Official Story, however, says: "left to their own devices, people are greedy and violent, etc". However, the greed and fear of scarcity is continually being generated by the monetary system, i.e. what one needs to do in order to have the money one needs to live. When our financial security is no longer a concern, we would indeed be free to pursue what motivates us.

Let us cultivate the consciousness that we can issue the money our capacities warrant, as an equity stake to create measurable value or as a grant to create unmeasurable value. Then one may begin to see that we could design society so that it will give us a just and sustainable abundance.

All of this now begs the question: What about the community? Don't we desire for ourselves what we desire for everyone? And don't we desire for everyone what we desire for ourselves? Don't we all desire to belong to a community in which our particular interests and skills are recognized and appreciated?

> *"Social life will be healthy when in the mirror of each human soul the community finds itself reflected, and when in the community the virtues and strengths of each one are living."*

Rudolf Steiner

"When a complex system is far from equilibrium, small islands of coherence in a sea of chaos have the capacity to shift the entire system to a higher order."

Ilya Prigogine, Nobel Prize-winning chemist

Sovereign individuals striving for self-awareness and transcendence are the small islands of coherence that have the potential to shift the chaos into the society we know in our hearts.

Now that we have looked at freedom, let us look at Justice, the basis for a worthy social compact.

Endnotes

See Just Abundance website for additional information on these topics

- For EndNotes: https://www.justabundance.org/fj
- Appendixes: https://www.justabundance.org/appendixes

Psychic Discoveries Behind the Iron Curtain

by Sheila Ostrander and Lynn Schroeder https://archive.org/details/psychic-discoveries-behind-the-sheila-ostrander

Remote Viewing

- https://en.wikipedia.org/wiki/Remote_viewing
- https://www.monroeinstitute.org/products/remote-viewing
- https://remoteviewingtraining.com/

Bruce Lipton

- *The Biology of Belief.* https://www.brucelipton.com/books/biology-of-belief/
- YouTube: https://www.youtube.com/watch?v=tj1O2K_HN3w

Lissa Rankin, MD

New York Times bestselling author of *The Daily Flame, Mind Over Medicine, The Fear Cure,* and *The Anatomy of a Calling.* She is an OB/GYN physician, author, keynote speaker, consultant to health care visionaries, professional artist, and founder of the women's health and wellness community Whole Health Medicine Institute.

- https://wholehealthmedicineinstitute.com/

- Amazon's website: <u>Mind Over Medicine - REVISED EDITION:</u> <u>Scientific Proof That You Can Heal Yourself - Kindle edition</u> <u>by Rankin, Lissa. Health, Fitness & Dieting Kindle eBooks @</u> <u>Amazon.com.</u>
- See her website: <u>http://LissaRankin.com</u>
- TEDtalk: <u>The shocking truth about your health | Lissa Rankin</u> <u>| TEDxFiDiWomen (youtube.com)</u>:

Jill Bolte Taylor, PhD

Dr. Jill Bolte Taylor is a Harvard-trained and published neuroanatomist whose research specialized in understanding how our brain creates our perception of reality.

- *My Stroke of Insight, A Brain Scientist's Personal Journey*
- *Whole Brain Living: The Anatomy of Choice and the Four Characters That Drive Our Life.*
- Ted Talk: <u>Bing Videos</u>

HeartMath

<u>https://www.heartmath.org/</u>

Joseph Chilton Pearce, Interview

Interview in Wild Duck Review: (<u>https://wildduckreviewarchives.</u> <u>wordpress.com/wp-content/uploads/2011/05/educationissue171.pdf</u>)

Handbook for the New Paradigm

- Book: <u>https://nohoax.net/index.php?option=com_content&</u> <u>view=article&id=24&catid=1</u>
- website: <u>https://nohoax.net</u>

Declaration of Independence

https://www.archives.gov/founding-docs/declaration-transcript

Grandmother Effect

https://www.statnews.com/2019/02/22/grandmother-effect-helps-explain-human-longevity/

Waldorf

https://www.waldorfeducation.org

Joseph Chilton Pearce

- *Evolution's End: Claiming the Potential of Our Intelligence,* pg 100-101
- *The Biology of Transcendence, pg 223-225*

John Taylor Gatto

John Taylor Gatto's, *Weapons of Mass Instruction: A Schoolteacher's Journey Through the Dark World of Compulsory Schooling,* focuses on mechanisms of traditional education which cripple imagination, discourage critical thinking, and create a false view of learning as a byproduct of rote-memorization drills.

Dan Pink

- Wikipedia on his book, *Drive: The Surprising Truth About What Motivates Us*: (https://en.wikipedia.org/wiki/Drive%3A_The_Surprising_Truth_About_What_Motivates_Us)

- The Video: https://www.youtube.com/watch?v=u6XAPnuFjJc
- USA Today Article: (https://usatoday30.usatoday.com/money/books/reviews/2010-01-25-drive25_ST_N.htm)

Transcendent Purpose

- From Google: "Transcendent purpose refers to a purpose or experience that goes beyond ordinary human existence. It is often associated with spiritual or philosophical concepts. Transcendent leadership involves commitment to a higher purpose, inspiring others to work towards a shared vision. In religious contexts, God is considered transcendent."
- Dr. Rob Archer, article "What Kind Of Purpose Leads To Meaning In Life?" published on the website for Working with Acceptance and Commitment Training (ACT). Posted on March 2, 2020 https://workingwithact.com/2020/03/02/what-kind-of-purpose-leads-to-meaning-in-life/

Ilya Prigogine

He is a Nobel Prize-winning chemist. The quote can be found in:

https://www.garrisoninstitute.org/islands-of-coherence/

THREE

Justice

"I think the first duty of society is justice."

Alexander Hamilton

"Justice, sir, is the great interest of man on earth. It is the ligament which holds civilized beings and civilized nations together."

Daniel Webster

"There is a higher court than courts of justice and that is the court of conscience. It supersedes all other courts."

Mahatma Gandhi

"Throughout history, it has been the inaction of those who could have acted; the indifference of those who should have known better; the silence of the voice of justice when it mattered most; that has made it possible for evil to triumph."

Haile Selassie

"Until the great mass of the people shall be filled with the sense of responsibility for each other's welfare, social justice can never be attained."

Helen Keller

These quotes resonate with most of us because human nature is such that we all desire our society to be just, i.e. everyone treated fairly. This is what we desire for ourselves and for everyone. Justice is administered according to law and, as far as the law is concerned, we are all equal.

Characteristics of <u>justice</u> include:

- The principle of moral rightness; decency;
- Conformity to moral rightness in action or attitude; righteousness;
- The attainment of what is just, especially that which is fair, moral, right, merited, or in accordance with law;
- the upholding of what is just, especially fair treatment and due reward in accordance with honor, standards, or law;
- the administration, system, methods, or procedures of law.
- Conformity to truth, fact, or sound reason:

In a society in which everything is a voluntary initiative and the individuals issue the money to measure the value they can be responsible for, the only real law needed is Do No Harm. When someone or a group is accused of doing harm, there must be a process whereby the community deals with the harm so that everyone will be able to feel that the process was fair, that justice was done, and that there was accountability for one's actions. Justice, after all, is what is required for us to associate with one another to achieve the good. Justice is the purpose of the social compact.

Everything that our heart knows as the society that benefits everyone is an aspect of justice. Our society will be just (and therefore peaceful and prosperous) when we take seriously our responsibility to govern ourselves - when we, the People, provide the governance.

Constitutions, laws, and courts fail to protect our rights for a very simple reason. They confer powers on government officials (judges, prosecutors, lawyers, police, legislators, governors, etc.) that the individual people do not have, such as the use of deadly force and the issuance of money. It is the acceptance of the idea of governmental authority being superior to individual authority that allows the abuses to continue and accumulate to tyranny. Larken Rose has a very good take on this. He states:

> "Most people have been so thoroughly trained to think that obedience is a virtue and that doing as you're told makes you a good person, that anything contrary to that can be very difficult for them to consider. But the truth is, being a moral person often requires disobeying so-called 'authorities' who use their power to exploit and dominate innocent people."

As Henry David Thoreau said, "If [the law] is of such a nature that it requires you to be the agent of injustice to another, then I say, break the law."

For society to be just, the people must be involved in administering justice. This is the origin of the English Common Law which was first codified in the Magna Carta, in the 1200's. Even the King needed to submit to the rule of law - the law that resides in the hearts and souls of the citizens. The Magna Carta is a significant document in the evolution of civil rights and is considered to be the first document of human freedom. It began the process that led to Parliament, and many centuries later to the American Revolution and the attempted transfer of full sovereignty from the King to the people.

Clause 39 still resonates today as one of the most powerful sentences in history: "No free man shall be seized or imprisoned, or stripped of his rights or possessions, or outlawed or exiled, or deprived of his standing in any other way, nor will we proceed with force against him, or send others to do so, except by the lawful judgment of his equals or by the law of the land."

Common Law, known to be the system of law originating in England, is based on custom, judicial decisions, or court decisions rather than civil law, ecclesiastical law, or statute law enacted by legislatures.

The key element of Common Law is the Jury made up of people from the district in which the harm happened, chosen by lot, (i.e. at random). It is the unanimous agreement of the jurors of the facts and the subsequent determination of the remedy, by the Jury that safeguards our rights.

When we commit to becoming self-directed, integrated, sovereign individuals, and when everything is becoming a voluntary initiative of committed people, then adjudicating and remedying harm is the main function of governance that we need.

Jural Assemblies

We can use Common Law and the Bill of Rights and the well-ordered Grand Jury and petit jury, to adjudicate and remedy harm. This may be accomplished by organizing our society that benefits everyone as Jural Assemblies. A Jural Assembly is the people who live in a particular defined place such as a town or city or county from which a jury (Grand Jury or petit jury) may be selected by lot. The Jural Assembly is the only political or 'governmental' organization that may authorize the use of force or compulsion and then only to adjudicate and remedy harm. In the society to benefit everyone, serving on a Jury when chosen by lot is the highest civic duty one may exercise. The oath of office as juror is to be honorable in administering justice and to determine the facts without sympathy or prejudice.

The belief that would unite the people in a Jural Assembly is simply this: "Do unto others as you would have others do unto you".

This is commonly known as the Golden Rule and is in virtually all religions:

1. Buddhism: *Hurt not others with that which pains yourself;*
2. Christianity: *Do unto others as you would have others do unto you.*
3. Hinduism: *Treat others as you yourself would be treated.*
4. Islam: *Do unto all men as you would wish to have done unto you.*
5. Judaism: *What you yourself hate, do to no man.*
6. Native American: *Live in harmony, for we are all related.*
7. Sacred Earth: *Do as you will, as long as you harm no one.*

There is only one natural law: Do no harm.

The Jury

Each State currently has a version of the Grand Jury. In Massachusetts the Grand Jury is made up of 23 people chosen from the voter roles and from the jurisdiction of the County Court. They are randomly chosen and serve at the pleasure of the State's Attorney General. It is very rare that a Grand Jury refuses to issue an indictment requested by the local attorney general.

Traditionally, it is the duty of the Grand Jury to determine if there is probable cause for an indictment or presentment when someone, a company, an organization, or group is accused of doing harm. An indictment by a Grand Jury accuses a person of a crime and a presentment accuses an organization or group of doing harm requiring further investigation. The indictment or presentment (also called a "true bill") sets due process in motion that leads to a trial by a Jury of 12 people chosen at random from the voter roles in the district where the harm occurred.

Traditionally, the Grand Jury determines only if the accusation is credible, based on an affidavit describing the harm and signed under penalty of perjury or based on their own suspicion of a crime having been committed. The Grand Jury has complete freedom to pursue whatever evidence they deem important. They have the power to subpoena witnesses and institute investigations in deciding whether to issue an indictment or presentment that would set in motion a circumstance that might require compulsion or deadly force to apprehend and compel attendance at a trial. The Grand Jury is only interested in making sure that an accusation is credible and worthy of initiating due process. They are not interested in any exculpatory evidence since it is the duty of the petit jury to determine the facts and issue a verdict.

Typically, the petit jury is composed of twelve people. They are chosen by lot or by random. Their oath is to determine the facts in a civil or criminal case, without favor or prejudice, and pronounce a verdict. Once they are unanimous about the facts of the matter, they announce or publish their determination or verdict. In the society that benefits everyone's proposed system, there will be no plea bargains and the petit jury will determine the just remedy as well.

There is a wonderful <u>decision of the Supreme Court from 1992</u> in which Antonin Scalia writes the opinion for the majority in a case that reaffirmed that the Grand Jury does not need to hear any exculpatory evidence since that is the job of the petit jury. What is so wonderful about the decision is that Scalia lays out the argument that the Grand Jury is an organ of the People, as in We, the People. It is a fundamental right of the people to come together, or 'assemble', as a Grand Jury to consider whether there is probable cause for a presentment or indictment. It is completely independent of the facilities of the Court that houses it. It is not a body subject to the authority of the Judges, or the Attorney's General; it is the fourth branch, the people's check on their government.

If the use of compulsion backed up by deadly force can only be carried out lawfully by the actions of a Grand Jury and a petit jury, then We, the People have one of the two key powers of the government in our hands. (The other key power is issuing the money.)

These ideas about organizing as a Jural Assembly and empowering juries to adjudicate harm are capable of manifesting the society we know in our hearts.

Nature of Justice

A jury from a Jural Assembly that sees itself as the protector of our unalienable rights as human beings would reject the idea behind the way a jury is instructed presently. An example of such an <u>instruction found on Wikipedia</u> follows:

> In the United States, a federal juror's oath usually states something to the effect of, "Do you and each of you solemnly swear that you will well and truly try and a true deliverance make between the United States and _____, the defendant at the bar, and a true verdict render according to the evidence, so help you God?"

Jury instructions sometimes make reference to the juror's oath. For example, the Criminal Pattern Jury Instructions developed by the U.S. Court of Appeals for the 10th Circuit for use by U.S. District Courts state:

> "You, as jurors, are the judges of the facts. But in determining what actually happened—that is, in reaching your decision as to the facts—it is your sworn duty to follow all of the rules of law as I explain them to you.
>
> You have no right to disregard or give special attention to any one instruction, or to question the wisdom or correctness of any rule I may state to you. You must not substitute or follow your own notion or opinion as to what the law is or ought to be. It is your duty to apply the law as I explain it to you, regardless of the consequences. However, you should not read into these instructions, or anything else I may have said or done, any suggestion as to what your verdict should be. That is entirely up to you.
>
> It is also your duty to base your verdict solely upon the evidence, without prejudice or sympathy. That was the promise you made and the oath you took."

These instructions to apply and adhere to the law and rule as stated by the judge are irrespective of the juror's opinion about the justice of said law and/or rule. Often the rules are about technicalities, the kind of technicalities that make a trial about winning and not about justice. It is entirely possible that the law and/or the rule is unjust and an aspect of the sick society that the powers-that-ought-not-to-be are implementing.

As Lysander Spooner stated: "It is not only the right and duty of juries to judge what are the facts, what is the law, and what was the moral intent of the accused; *but that it is also their right, and their primary and paramount duty, to judge of the justice of the law, and to hold all laws invalid, that are, in their opinion, unjust or oppressive, and all persons guiltless in violating, or resisting the execution of, such laws."*

In the better world, the jurors must use their own judgment about justice to evaluate the meaning of the facts as well as the justice of the law(s). And when determining the just remedy, the jurors would need to be aware of Retributive Justice, Restorative Justice, and Distributive Justice.

Retributive Justice

Retributive Justice, which is the only "justice" in today's legal system, focuses solely on the punishment of the offender, rather than rehabilitation or deterrence. In biblical times, retribution was based on the principle of equal and direct retribution, expressed in Exodus 21:24 as "an eye for an eye." The theory behind retributive justice is that when people commit crimes, "justice" requires that they be punished in return and that the severity of their punishment should be proportionate to the seriousness of their crime. Punishment of the crime (even victimless crimes) is generally in the form of fines or jail time. Occasionally there is compensation for victims, such as the offender paying restitution. And in some states (and countries), the punishment for causing death is death.

Plea bargaining in the United States is very common; the vast majority of criminal cases (90% of the convictions) in the United States are settled by plea bargain rather than by a jury trial. Supposedly, a plea bargain allows both parties to avoid a lengthy criminal trial and may allow criminal defendants to avoid the risk of conviction in a trial on a more serious charge. Plea bargains are an admission of guilt, whether guilty or not, but for a less serious crime with less jail time or a smaller fine than if there was a conviction in a trial by jury. For example, a criminal defendant charged with a felony theft charge, the conviction of which would require imprisonment in state prison, may be offered the opportunity to plead guilty to a misdemeanor theft charge, which may not carry a custodial sentence.

However, the plea bargain system is not without its critics. John H. Langbein argues that the modern American system of plea bargaining is comparable to the medieval European system of torture: "There is, of course, a difference between having your limbs crushed if you refuse to confess, or suffering some extra years of imprisonment if you refuse to confess, but the difference is of degree, not kind. Plea bargaining, like torture, is coercive. Like the medieval Europeans, the Americans are now operating a procedural system that engages in condemnation without adjudication."

Plea bargains are based on the uncertainty of a jury trial. This uncertainty can be because the jury trial is not guaranteed to be a trial by a jury of one's peers. Rather, it can be based on a jury selected from the pool to be most easily manipulated by competing lawyers.

Retributive Justice does not create a just society nor reduce crime. The adversarial system of justice, the competition between the Prosecuting Attorney and the Defense Attorney, and the fallibility of judges make it all about winning, and not about justice. The court system is not concerned with justice. In fact, the "justice" system appears to be perversely inclined to send people to prison, regardless of the consequences for society. The United States has among the highest per capita prison population in the world and rigorous scientific studies have shown it does not reduce crime, or make us safer.

Restorative Justice

"We are breaking cycles of trauma by promoting and strengthening alternative responses to violence. When we succeed, we will

transform justice from a system of punishment and harm to one of healing, equity, and genuine accountability. Justice, Reimagined.˙

- Equal Justice USA

There is a growing movement that desires to heal rather than punish. Healing is justice that corresponds to the sentiment, "what I desire for myself is what I desire for everyone else. If I commit a crime, I desire to be able to remedy the harm I have done. I would like everyone to have the opportunity to remedy the harm their crime has created".

Restorative Justice is well developed and well represented at the National Association of Community and Restorative Justice, Restorative Justice Exchange, and Equal Justice USA. There are many inspiring stories about the unique ways in which justice is achieved. Here is an excerpt from the Restorative Justice website:

"The Heart of the Matter

Crime and wrongdoing break down individual relationships, but the ripple effect of those behaviors can extend the impact to include friends, families, communities and many others. While crime causes broken relationships, it also flows from broken relationships and communities. Crime occurs within a context of deeper hurts, power imbalances, and unjust structures. Often, we at Prison Fellowship International (PFI) find that we must dig down further to uncover the initial hurts that have been ignored, suppressed or not recognized. We must give these wounds the light and attention they need to properly heal.

Justice, like crime, ripples outward. It leads to wholeness and wellbeing within us, our relationships, our communities, and our world. Like fishermen who mend their nets in the morning after fishing all night, justice requires that those most impacted by crime do the hard work of mending the torn nets of their relationships.

We recognize that Justice should also address the root causes of crime, even to the point of transforming unjust systems and structures. If restorative justice is based on the idea that we are interconnected and woven together in humanity's netting, then we must examine and actively address the underlying issues that lead to crime and the context in which it occurs.

With this in mind, we define restorative justice as:
A response to wrongdoing that prioritizes repairing harm, to the extent possible, caused or revealed by the wrongful behavior. The stakeholders impacted most by the wrongdoing cooperatively decide how to repair victim harm, hold offenders accountable and strengthen the community's relational health and safety.

How Crime Hurts Everyone
Broken criminal justice systems help perpetuate the cycle of crime.

Lengthy Pre-Trial Detention
Millions of prisoners around the world are held in crowded, inhumane conditions as they wait for trial. Often, they wait longer than the maximum sentence they could receive if found guilty.

Punitive Punishment
Many justice systems focus on punishment for wrongdoings rather than creating rehabilitative environments where prisoners can learn personal responsibility for their behavior. (Some of PFI's greatest contributions to restorative justice occur in the incarceration stage, reshaping prisoners' experiences to be transformative rather than simply punitive.)

Suffering Victims

Victims of crime receive little help to recover from their trauma. They are ignored except when called as a witness in a prosecution.

Silent Victims

Families and children of prisoners live in poverty in remote, hard-to-reach communities. They are often ostracized for being related to a prisoner and are at risk for physical harm and emotional trauma.

How Restorative Justice Repairs Harm

Restorative justice is best accomplished through cooperative processes that allow willing prisoners and victims to meet and explore topics such as personal responsibility and making amends. This can lead to the transformation of people, relationships, and communities.

Learn how this transformation is taking place in first-person accounts of the impact of PFI's restorative justice work through our global network of practitioners."

Restorative justice has been growing in use in criminal cases in the US. Here is an example of how a homicide victim's family chose reconciliation over a life sentence in the aftermath of a 2016 North Carolina murder:

... the facts are not in dispute. Donald Fields Jr., then 24 years old, pulled out a pocket knife and stabbed his father, Donald Sr., during a heated argument that began over the placement of a TV in their home.

Gutted, the family initially turned away from Fields Jr. and left the justice system to respond in its usual ways. But after some time, multiple family members, led by Fields' uncle Alex, embraced a restorative justice approach — an alternative to the traditional trial and sentencing process that includes dialogue between victims and offenders. That process transformed the tragedy into what Laughland described as a "pioneering case of compassion in America's punitive criminal justice system."

Fields Jr. initially faced a possible sentence of life in prison. Instead, after a lengthy and involved process of reconciliation and accountability, he was released after six years in jail.

There are additional stories available on restorative justice websites. Many of the stories illustrate our true nature, as "in love your neighbor as yourself", showing how crime is a cry for help and what may happen when help is forthcoming.

Distributive Justice

There are different views about how to achieve a fair distribution of the benefits and wealth of society. In the Official Story, there are two distinct versions: capitalism and communism. In capitalism, the rights of capital are prioritized and labor is denigrated (human resources are bought and paid for with money). In communism, the rights of labor are prioritized and the rights of capital are denigrated (the money belongs to us all and the state will distribute it as it sees fit). These are both lies. Capitalism ignores the role of banks in creating money and how the banks automatically transfer the wealth from the "human resources" that create the wealth with their labor to the owners of the banks. Communism ignores the role of their independent central bank in funding the state, maintaining the inefficiencies of a command economy, and undermining private initiative. Capitalism does not create distributive justice, it creates monopolies and government capture, i.e. a corporatocracy. Communist distribution tramples human freedom and stifles creativity. Both capitalism and communism deny our essential humanity and distort the justice that lives in the hearts and souls of the people.

The Justice that is written in our hearts and souls desires that everyone be in a position to recognize and manifest their transcendent purpose in life. This requires that people are capitalized to the full extent of their capacities and that the people who are incapable of contributing to society by virtue of a disability or old age are supported to live a dignified life.

People are not money-motivated when they have the right amount of money to do what they feel called to do, to fulfill their calling in life. This is described in great detail in Dan Pink's book *Drive: The Surprising Truth About What Motivates Us*, where he states that human motivation is largely intrinsic and that the aspects of this motivation can be divided into autonomy, mastery, and purpose. This insight has come to be called the Purpose Economy. The Purpose Economy is a phrase coined by Aaron Hurst to describe the way in which work is changing to reflect the desire amongst employees to realize a higher societal purpose in their work. The theory of the Purpose Economy suggests that companies will be more successful in the long-term only if they have a very clear sense of societal purpose, with which employees can closely identify.

The practical consequence is that everyone must be both a capitalist with a voice in management and a laborer with an equity stake. The Purpose Economy prioritizes both capital and labor. The workers must also be capitalists to participate worthily in their destinies.

Money can only ever be issued for consumption or production. If issued for consumption, it is issued as a grant; if issued for production, it is issued as an investment as an equity stake. Regulating the money supply means making sure that there is the right amount of money available to ensure equitable distribution, i.e. justice. Justice requires that people have access to the right amount of money for them to achieve their life's purpose.

In a Jural Assembly dedicated to the Golden Rule and Do No Harm, everyone is in a position to issue the money they need to capitalize their capacities and collaborate with other capitalized individuals to accomplish a common purpose. The capitalized laborers decide how to distribute the profits based on their sense of justice. In Jural Assemblies, everyone participates by what they voluntarily do to create distributive justice.

To adjudicate harm responsibly, it is imperative that the people in every Jural Assembly have an awareness of restorative and distributive justice as well as be familiar with the Laws of Nature and of Nature's God, the Bill of Rights, the Maxims of Law, and Maxims of Equity.

A Bit of History

"...to be strictly just, [the authority of government] must have the sanction and consent of the governed. It can have no pure right over my person and property but what I concede to it."

- Henry David Thoreau in his essay "Civil Disobedience"

The Declaration of Independence set the stage for the Revolution and the Constitution. The Constitution could not be ratified as written because it did not include strict protection for the inherent rights of the people, harking back to English Common Law. Specifically, it did not identify the rights of the people independent of the government. It did not make explicit how the people were to go about consenting. The Constitution was ratified when it was amended to include the Bill of Rights, which had the effect of including Common Law in the Constitution. Common law due process and trial by a jury of one's peers is enshrined in the Bill of Rights.

Our expectation of a just society originates with the expectation of the Colonists that they were Englishmen and thus protected by English Common Law. Colonial Scrip gave the Colonists a real experience of creating their own fortune, but the revocation of their homegrown money created the social conditions which fostered the rebellion.

The Continental Congress enabled its participants to experience their sovereignty. They went from being loyal subjects of Britain to being loyal to each other in their quest for the liberty to continue creating their own fortunes. Among the first acts of the Continental Congress was issuing Continentals. The members of the Congress experienced themselves as sovereign. They did what the sovereign always does - they issued money to create the conditions in which they desired to live. Later, in the Second Continental Congress, its members realized that they would have to separate from Britain to create the conditions they saw as good and necessary. This required the Declaration of Independence. This is well described by Alexander del Mar, in his book, *The History of Money in America from the Earliest Times to the Establishment of the Constitution.*

Today our relationship with our government is similar to the Colonists relationship with their King. We will either continue to suffer from our loyalty to the Government or we will need to commit to each other and repudiate our Government.

Declaration of Independence

The <u>Declaration of Independence</u> is an expression of simple, foundational truths. Being familiar with its message will surely guide us in realizing its promise and help us create the just world we know in our hearts.

1. It begins with the three-step remedy for tyranny as an introduction and outline of the document:

    When in the Course of human events, it becomes necessary for one people (1) to dissolve the political bands which have connected them with another, and (2) to assume among the powers of the earth, the separate and equal station to which the Laws of Nature and of Nature's God entitle them, a decent respect to the opinions of mankind requires that they should (3) declare the causes which impel them to the separation.

2. It continues with a description of the rights inherent in human nature:

    We hold these truths to be self-evident, that all men are created equal, that they are endowed by their Creator with certain unalienable Rights, that among these are Life, Liberty and the pursuit of Happiness.

3. Next is a straightforward, simple statement about consent as the essence of a just social compact:

    —That to secure these rights, Governments are instituted among Men, deriving their just powers from the consent of the governed, —

4. Then it states the goal of the social compact:

    That whenever any Form of Government becomes destructive of these ends, it is the Right of the People to alter or to abolish it, and to institute new Government, laying its foundation on such principles and organizing its powers in such form, as to them shall seem most likely to effect their Safety and Happiness.

5. Followed by an acknowledgment of the inertia inherent in human nature:

    Prudence, indeed, will dictate that Governments long established should not be changed for light and transient causes; and accordingly all experience hath shewn, that mankind are more disposed to suffer, while evils are sufferable, than to right themselves by abolishing the forms to which they are accustomed.

6. and the urgency to recognize tyranny and the duty to create a new social compact:

    But when a long train of abuses and usurpations, pursuing invariably the same Object evinces a design to reduce them under absolute Despotism, it is their right, it is their duty, to throw off such Government, and to provide new Guards for their future security..—Such has been the patient sufferance of these Colonies; and such is now the necessity which constrains them to alter their former Systems of Government.

7. Based on these facts of tyranny:

The history of the present King of Great Britain is a history of repeated injuries and usurpations, all having in direct object the establishment of an absolute Tyranny over these States. To prove this, let Facts be submitted to a candid world.

[The List of grievances follow]

In every stage of these Oppressions we have Petitioned for Redress in the most humble terms: Our repeated Petitions have been answered only by repeated injury. A Prince, whose character is thus marked by every act which may define a Tyrant, is unfit to be the Ruler of a free People.

Nor have We been wanting in attentions to our British brethren. We have warned them from time to time of attempts by their Legislature to extend an unwarrantable jurisdiction over us. We have reminded them of the circumstances of our emigration and settlement here. We have appealed to their native justice and magnanimity, and we have conjured them by the ties of our common kindred to disavow these usurpations, which, would inevitably interrupt our connections and correspondence. They too have been deaf to the voice of justice and of consanguinity. We must, therefore, acquiesce in the necessity, which denounces our Separation, and hold them, as we hold the rest of mankind, Enemies in War, in Peace Friends.

8. Representing with pure intention the people:

That these United Colonies are, and of Right ought to be Free and Independent States; that they are Absolved from all Allegiance to the British Crown, and that all political connection between them and the State of Great Britain, is and ought to be totally dissolved;

9. The political bands are dissolved:

    and that as Free and Independent States, they have full Power to levy War, conclude Peace, contract Alliances, establish Commerce, and to do all other Acts and Things which Independent States may of right do.

10. Full power is assumed to create a new social compact:

    And for the support of this Declaration, with a firm reliance on the protection of divine Providence, we mutually pledge to each other our Lives, our Fortunes and our sacred Honor.

11. As evidenced by the commitment of the signers:

    It was signed by the assembled delegates to the Continental Congress.

The list of signers are grouped by state. For example, for Massachusetts, Samuel Adams, John Adams, Robert Treat Paine, and Elbridge Gerrty signed the Declaration.

Our grievances would be very similar, but we would add the following items which have become "business as usual":

- the Money Power,
- the lawyers and judges that protect the banking fraud,
- the Deep State and the American Empire,
- debt and wage slavery,
- the loss of privacy and other basic rights,
- no opportunity for active consent nor withdrawal of consent,
- no redress of grievances,
- the existence of monopolies,
- secular humanism or scientism as the State Religion, and
- the technocratic transhumanist totalitarian tiptoe.

Preamble to the Massachusetts Constitution

To understand the importance of the social compact, the <u>Preamble to the Massachusetts Constitution</u> can be helpful. The Constitution was written by John Adams, and adopted by the town meetings in 1780. It is the oldest written constitution still governing in the world.

"The end [purpose] of the institution, maintenance, and administration of government, is to secure the existence of the body politic, to protect it, and to furnish the individuals who compose it with the power of enjoying in safety and tranquility their natural rights, and the blessings of life: and whenever these great objects are not obtained, the people have a right to alter the government, and to take measures necessary for their safety, prosperity and happiness.

The body politic is formed by a voluntary association of individuals: it is a social compact, by which the whole people covenants with each citizen, and each citizen with the whole people, that all shall be governed by certain laws for the common good. It is the duty of the people, therefore, in framing a constitution of government, to provide for an equitable mode of making laws, as well as for an impartial interpretation, and a faithful execution of them; that every man may, at all times, find his security in them.

We, therefore, the people of Massachusetts, acknowledging, with grateful hearts, the goodness of the great Legislator of the universe, in affording us, in the course of His providence, an opportunity, deliberately and peaceably, without fraud, violence or surprise, of entering into an original, explicit, and solemn compact with each other; and of forming a new constitution of civil government, for ourselves and posterity; and devoutly imploring His direction in so interesting a design, do agree upon, ordain and establish the following Declaration of Rights, and Frame of Government, as the Constitution of the Commonwealth of Massachusetts."

The first part of the Constitution of the Commonwealth of Massachusetts is the Declaration of Rights for an inhabitant of the Commonwealth. The Frame of Government Section sets up the separation of powers that we are familiar with: Legislative, Executive, and Judicial Powers. Unfortunately, the Constitution of the Commonwealth of Massachusetts has *not* led to a society that benefits everyone.

The Bill of Rights

The U.S. Constitution was ratified when it was amended to include the Bill of Rights, which had the effect of including Common Law in the Constitution. Below are those first 10 amendments to the 1787 Constitution for the United States of America, better known as the Bill of Rights. The bolded sections indicate a specific reference to the customs of Common Law.

Amendment I - Freedom of Religion, Speech, and the Press

Congress shall make no law respecting an establishment of religion, or prohibiting the free exercise thereof; or abridging the freedom of speech, or of the press; ***or the right of the people peaceably to assemble, and to petition the Government for a redress of grievances.***

Amendment II - The Right to Bear Arms

A well regulated Militia, being necessary to the security of a free State, the right of the people to keep and bear Arms, shall not be infringed.

Amendment III - The Housing of Soldiers

No Soldier shall, in time of peace be quartered in any house, without the consent of the Owner, nor in time of war, but in a manner to be prescribed by law.

Amendment IV - Protection from Unreasonable Searches and Seizures

The right of the people to be secure in their persons, houses, papers, and effects, against unreasonable searches and seizures, shall not be violated, and no Warrants shall issue, but upon probable cause, supported by Oath or affirmation, and particularly describing the place to be searched, and the persons or things to be seized.

Amendment V - Protection of Rights to Life, Liberty, and Property

No person shall be held to answer for a capital, or otherwise infamous crime, unless on a presentment or indictment of a Grand Jury, *except in cases arising in the land or naval forces, or in the Militia, when in actual service in time of War or public danger;* **nor shall any person be subject for the same offence to be twice put in jeopardy of life or limb; nor shall be compelled in any criminal case to be a witness against himself, nor be deprived of life, liberty, or property, without due process of law; nor shall private property be taken for public use, without just compensation.**

Amendment VI - Rights of Accused Persons in Criminal Cases

In all criminal prosecutions, the accused shall enjoy the right to a speedy and public trial, by an impartial jury of the State and district wherein the crime shall have been committed, which district shall have been previously ascertained by law, and to be informed of the nature and cause of the accusation; to be confronted with the witnesses against him; to have compulsory process for obtaining witnesses in his favor, and to have the Assistance of Counsel for his defence.

Amendment VII - Rights in Civil Cases

In Suits at common law, where the value in controversy shall exceed twenty dollars, the right of trial by jury shall be preserved, and no fact tried by a jury, shall be otherwise re-examined in any Court of the United States, than according to the rules of the common law.

Amendment VIII - Excessive Bail, Fines, and Punishments Forbidden

Excessive bail shall not be required, nor excessive fines imposed, nor cruel and unusual punishments inflicted.

Amendment IX - Other Rights Kept by the People

The enumeration in the Constitution, of certain rights, shall not be construed to deny or disparage others retained by the people.

Amendment X - Undelegated Powers Kept by the States and the People

The powers not delegated to the United States by the Constitution, nor prohibited by it to the States, are reserved to the States respectively, or to the people.

The Uniform Commercial Code

What has happened to Common Law? In Common Law, the banking cartel's loan contract is unconscionable because of the various deceptions involved. To continue its hegemony, the banking cartel had to eviscerate common law. They brought the Law of the Sea onto the land and usurped the Common Law.

Historically, commerce was regulated by <u>Maritime Law or Admiralty Law</u>, the Law of the Sea, which is based on enforcing the terms of the contract no matter how egregious those terms may be. On the Sea, because there is no sovereign or lawgiver to enforce the law, Admiralty

Courts or tribunals were set up in the major ports by the British Empire to hear the disputes regarding the contracts on the seas. Because there was no sovereign, as there is on the land and therefore no possibility of justice, only the terms of the contract and whether or not they were adhered to were pertinent. Since banking is represented fraudulently and the banking contract for "lending" is unconscionable, it was necessary for the powers-that-ought-not-to-be to overcome the common sense of Common Law.

The Uniform Commercial Code is the result. Here are the list of articles contained within it:

- U.C.C. - ARTICLE 1 - GENERAL PROVISIONS (2001)
- U.C.C. - ARTICLE 2 - SALES (2002)
- U.C.C. - ARTICLE 2A - LEASES (2002)
- U.C.C. - ARTICLE 3 - NEGOTIABLE INSTRUMENTS (2002)
- U.C.C. - ARTICLE 4 - BANK DEPOSITS AND COLLECTIONS (2002)
- U.C.C. - ARTICLE 4A - FUNDS TRANSFER (2012)
- U.C.C. - ARTICLE 5 - LETTERS OF CREDIT (1995)
- REPEALER OF U.C.C. - ARTICLE 6 - BULK TRANSFERS and [REVISED] U.C.C. - ARTICLE 6 - BULK SALES (1989)
- U.C.C. - ARTICLE 7 - DOCUMENTS OF TITLE (2003)
- U.C.C. - ARTICLE 8 - INVESTMENT SECURITIES (1994)
- U.C.C. - ARTICLE 9 - SECURED TRANSACTIONS (2010)
- UCC - older versions

Article 3 relates to checks, drafts, and other negotiable instruments, such as a note (a promise to pay money). An item is considered negotiable if it can be transferred to another individual and still be enforceable against the original payer.

Here is what the UCC says, in part, about negotiable instruments:

3-104. NEGOTIABLE INSTRUMENT.

(a) Except as provided in subsections (c) and (d), "**negotiable instrument**" means an unconditional promise or order to pay a fixed amount of money, with or without interest or other charges described in the promise or order, if it:

(1) is payable to bearer or to order at the time it is issued or first comes into possession of a holder;

(2) is payable on demand or at a definite time; and

(3) does not state any other undertaking or instruction by the person promising or ordering payment to do any act in addition to the payment of money, but the promise or order may contain (i) an undertaking or power to give, maintain, or protect collateral to secure payment, (ii) an authorization or power to the holder to confess judgment or realize on or dispose of collateral, or (iii) a waiver of the benefit of any law intended for the advantage or protection of an obligor.

Here is an excerpt from Uniform Law Commission regarding its summary of the Article 3:

Negotiable instruments make the economy go around.... What is a negotiable instrument? It is either a draft, of which the most common subcategory is the check, or a note....A note is evidence of a debt between the maker, who promises to pay, and another person. A traditional promissory note is an example. One person borrows money from another person. The borrower signs a piece of paper that obligates him to pay the money back at a certain time. That piece of paper, which evidences the debt, is a note.

The UCC defines "Person" to mean an individual, corporation, business trust, estate, trust, partnership, limited liability company, association, joint venture, government, governmental subdivision, agency, or instrumentality, public corporation, or any other legal or commercial entity.

The way this is worded, we will assume that a bank is a person. This is the law supporting the fraudulent banking contract

In Common Law, the *intent* of the contract governs, not the wording. In the UCC, the *wording* governs and not the intent. The banking contract is unconscionable because the intent of the banking cartel is to deceive the "borrower" by making it seem as though banks are lending money that is theirs to lend.

If we knew that the bank is "lending" what it owes us, we would make the case in a Common Law court that there is no consideration and the contract is void. Consideration is a promise, performance, or forbearance bargained by a promisor in exchange for their promise. Consideration is the main element of a contract. Without consideration by both parties, a contract cannot be enforceable. The banker's consideration is not the bankers to lend since we created the value with our promise to pay. Therefore the contract is void, our promise to pay is unenforceable and the house is ours since we are providing the value. We created the value of the house; the house is ours, not the bank's.

In the better world, the money to pay for a house would not be provided with a loan, it would be provided through a grant by the community, we, the people.

To summarize, the UCC makes the wording of the contract the controlling issue. It says "a note is an unconditional promise or order to pay". It does not matter how often anyone proves that the banking contract is fraudulent, you signed a promissory note that says you owe principal and interest in an amortized monthly payment. You have no recourse to a Common Law court, a trial by jury, or any other remedy. The best that Congress has been able to do is recommend that banks offer to modify the payments when you can't pay.

Reading the UCC gives one a good sense for how the UCC protects banks by enforcing the letter of the banking contracts and not the intention or the spirit of the contracts. Reading the <u>Maxims of Law</u> and the <u>Maxims of Equity</u> gives a very different experience of the law. Every one of them make sense and are helpful in thinking about how best to serve justice.

Congress is so captured by the banking cartel that it is not reasonable to believe that Congress could challenge the banking monopoly to restore its right to issue the currency.

The Official Story says that we withdraw our consent by voting "the bums out" and voting for those candidates we most agree with and whom we expect will redress our grievances. Clearly, this process has not worked for a long time! We all have had the experience of choosing between the lesser of two evils, or of voting for the hero who has no chance of winning (a "spoiler"), and draws votes from the lesser of the two evils we favored.

This is exactly what is happening now. Supporters of Donald Trump are wildly enthusiastic about him - he is a populist who says he will protect our rights and liberties, and Make America Great Again (MAGA); Joe Biden's support is lukewarm at best, from traditional Democrats who believe the Official Story and are fearful of Donald Trump winning. Robert Kennedy Jr is the hero, the one whose life story includes taking on the mega companies that have captured the Media and the Government Agencies meant to regulate them, and winning - holding them to account. If one is a Democrat and would like to vote for Kennedy, one can't because then Trump would win. If one is a Republican and would like to vote for Kennedy, one can't because then Biden would win. Voting creates winners and losers and big money decides who the candidates will be. The likes of <u>Marrianne Williamson</u>, with thoughtful, responsible, and transformative messages, do not even get a stage, whatsoever. Also, although there are two parties in the culture wars, there is but one Uniparty when it comes to supporting the Agenda of the Military Industrial, Banking, and Pharmaceutical Complex.

What is interesting is that the hero scenario has been going on since I became active in electoral politics in 1968 and campaigned for Eugene McCarthy - the peace candidate - after Robert Kennedy Sr was assassinated. This meant that the democratic vote was split, so Nixon (tricky Dick) won.

<u>Étienne de La Boétie</u> (1530 – 1563), a French magistrate, classicist, writer, poet and political theorist, had an interesting perspective on consent. His early political essay, *Discourse on Voluntary Servitude*, is a current influence on modern anti-statist, utopian, and civil disobedience thought. Since our compliance is what the tyrant relies on, we withdraw our consent by not complying. <u>Etienne de la Boetie2</u>, the founder of the Art of Liberty Foundation, has taken up his mantle to show us the illegitimacy and criminality of "government" from a principled voluntarist perspective. In his book, *"Government" - The Biggest Scam in History... Exposed!* he makes the case that the Government is illegitimate and was never intended to protect life, liberty, and property, but has always been used by inter-generational organized crime to rob and enslave.

Justice Resides in the Hearts and Souls of the People

"Justice in the life and conduct of the State is possible only as first it resides in the hearts and souls of the citizens."

Plato

"The idea nearest to my heart is that the people learn to provide the functions of government to each other."

Thomas Jefferson

"Must the citizen ever for a moment, or in the least degree, resign his conscience to the legislator? Why has every man a conscience then? I think that we should be men first, and subjects afterward.

There will never be a really free and enlightened State until the State comes to recognize the individual as a higher and independent power, from which all its own power and authority are derived, and treats him accordingly."

Henry David Thoreau in his essay "Civil Disobedience"

The idea that justice resides in the hearts and souls of the people allows us to have confidence that we create justice in the better world. We can exercise our right of assembly to form Jural Assemblies, convene Grand Juries and petit juries, begin the process of righting the wrongs we have become accustomed to, and create the new reality that is our true birthright.

After his Presidency, Jefferson wrote about what he called the "Ward Republic" in some of his letters. He proposed that the <u>Ward Republic</u> be based on the ability of people to meet together, in person, where they live, and reason with each other to create the social conditions in which they desire to live. Harking back to the Middle Ages in England after 1066, ten families would choose a Tithingman to be responsible for bringing anyone of them who were accused of causing harm to the King's court.

The Old Testament is a source of this custom, for example in Exodus 18:21: *"Moreover thou shalt provide out of all the people able men, such as fear God, men of truth, hating covetousness; and place such over them, to be rulers of thousands, and rulers of hundreds, rulers of fifties, and rulers of* tens." And in Deuteronomy 1:15: *"So I took the chief of your tribes, wise men, and known, and made them heads over you, captains over thousands, and captains over hundreds, and captains over fifties, and captains over tens, and officers among your tribes."*

In Jefferson's conception, ten families make a Hundred, which is a Ward; ten Wards make a Village, which is Thousands; Ten Villages make a Town, which is Tens of Thousands; ten Towns make a City or County, which is a Hundred Thousands, and on up through the States, to the Nation and beyond. Every significant decision affecting the family, the Ward, the Village, the Town, the City, the County, the State, or the Nation is actively consented to by the families in the Wards affected. There shall be no compulsion or coercion! And especially, there shall be no "silence is consent". The belief in authority, that one must obey the law, over the objections of one's conscience, is the belief that the Ward Republic is intended to overcome.

To be just, governance requires our consent. Creating active consent-based, self-governing Jural Assembly communities in the context of the Ward Republic gives us the best prospect of manifesting our desire for justice.

Active consent is always possible when it is based on certain underlying realities of human nature, namely our social nature. We are social beings. We come together to enjoy each other's company, in family gatherings, formally in a meeting, or informally in a social gathering, such as a block party, club, or church.

We come together because we are part of a family, because of a common interest or activity, or because we are responding to a call for a gathering to accomplish something we believe in and desire to participate in. Family gatherings aim to renew our connections with the people we raised or grew up with and to maintain family harmony. In our current culture, it is important to avoid talking about money, politics, or religion, i.e. all the topics the elite use to divide and conquer. But if we are responding to an aim or purpose that we resonate with, the conversation will likely be about money, politics, or religion.

If we respond to the aim to create the society that benefits everyone, the world we know in our hearts is possible, the ideal social future, realizing the promise of the Declaration of Independence, etc, we will meet to discuss *specifically* money, politics, and religion. We will want to meet face to face and get to know the other people who have a similar aim. We will share our vision of the ideal society, and by doing so, we will be in the process of creating it.

What is necessary to create the social conditions where our lives are secure so that we are at liberty to pursue the transcendent purpose we feel called to serve, which is the most reliable basis for our happiness?

We may readily agree that the basis for a just society is our recognition that the rights we desire for ourselves are also what we desire for everyone. We desire to be properly capitalized (i.e. have the money) so that our lives are secure and we are at Liberty to pursue the transcendent purpose that gives us the most joy.

If this is our aim, then that aim is the guiding principle. We will evaluate all the proposals or policies developed in accordance with how well they support the aim. We know from our experience that everyone who is drawn to the aim will have different ideas about how to implement it. Therefore, if we hear from everyone, all the ideas we need to benefit the community will be on the table. If everyone has confidence that they will be heard, then listening to each other is easy. Consequently, we will always go in a "round", hearing from each person in the circle. In this way, everyone has the opportunity to respond to what is being said when it is their turn.

We also need to agree that we will ground our ideas in terms that are well-reasoned and accessible to discussion. For example, "I don't like it" is not good enough. Everyone must be able to describe what they find objectionable using a rational argument. Hearing from everyone and committing to accepting help to express our thoughts and feelings in terms that are accessible to discussion are key values for active consent-based governance.

Most objections to a proposal or policy stem from a concern about unintended consequences. Therefore, every proposal or policy must have a method of evaluating it and the timeframe for that evaluation. Integrating the concern that leads to the objection into the proposal or policy will improve it. Strengthening the criteria by which it will be evaluated and shortening or lengthening the time frame when it will be evaluated will lead to a willingness to consent to it. The question often becomes: "Is it good enough for now and safe enough to try?"

Voting creates winners and losers, which is the very definition of *not* benefiting everyone. Therefore, in the society we create together, we will select the best person for a role. Who would be best suited to lead the project, to facilitate the meetings, to keep the records, or to represent our group?

The Leader needs to be someone who has a clear vision of the aim and can keep the group inspired to accomplish its aim. The Facilitator makes sure the meetings are well run and productive, that everyone is heard from, that the proposals are well presented, and is someone who can come up with creative ways to solve conundrums that inevitably come up in meetings. The Scribe or record keeper is responsible for the minutes of the meetings and other documentation and making sure that all the members of the group have access to such, know when evaluations are coming up, and how to contribute to the Agenda for meetings. The Delegate will represent the group in other groups, especially the ones in neighboring Districts or Wards.

There is a particularly well-developed system of consent-based self-governance called Dynamic Governance or <u>Sociocracy</u>.

"It is a theory of governance that seeks to create psychologically safe environments and productive organizations. It draws on the use of consent, rather than majority voting, in discussion and decision-making by people who have a shared goal or work process."

- Wikipedia

"Sociocracy is a governance system, just like democracy or corporate governance methods. It's best suited for organizations that want to self-govern based on the values of equality."

- Sociocracy for All,

Sociocracy is a social movement - the infrastructure for the new society - that we believe is best represented by the organization, Sociocracy for All, and by Ted Rau and Jerry Koch Gonzales. Their organization provides training and a community of practice that caters to every level of interest and commitment.

The Social Compact

The Social Compact described in this chapter keeps political power with the people, bottom-up in their Ward and Jural Assembly. The Jural Assembly ensures that the people are never required by the social compact to submit to an injustice because it is their sense of justice that governs.

Justice requires that sovereignty be with the individual and administered by the people. Issuing money and adjudicating and remediating harm are the primary responsibilities of the sovereign.

Imagine the following:

In the society that benefits everyone, we readily agree that:

- The only law is Do No Harm.
- The Jural Assembly is based on the Golden Rule and is responsible for adjudicating and remediating harm.
- The only requirement is one will show up when selected at random for Jury Duty.
- The jury is chosen by a random selection process and is representative of the general population in the city or county jurisdiction from where it was established.
- The jury will use their best judgment regarding the facts of the matter being adjudicated and,
- In a separate proceeding, the jury will decide the just remedy, using their vision and their understanding of retributive, restorative, and distributive justice.

When there is general confidence in the process which adjudicates harm, and that process is reflective of the values cultivated in the community in which the harm happened, people will feel safe.

When everything that happens is a voluntary initiative of individuals collaborating to provide everything that any one of them, and every one, reasonably desires, the community will flourish.

When the individuals undertaking a voluntary initiative have the right to the capital their capacities warrant, the community will be prosperous.

This is the essence of justice, that everyone is free to pursue their transcendent purpose as they see fit, and everything is based on merit and the recognition of particular capacities and good ideas.

This fulfills the promise of the Declaration of Independence. Everyone's Life is secure because they may issue the money to capitalize their capacities. As a result, everyone is at Liberty to Pursue their life's purpose, which is the only true source of Happiness. Life, Liberty, and the pursuit of Happiness are realized.

How these ideas might be implemented will be the subject of the Fifth Chapter, but first we need to understand our desire for Community.

Endnotes

See Just Abundance website for additional information on these topics

- For EndNotes: https://www.justabundance.org/fj
- Appendixes: https://www.justabundance.org/appendixes

Justice

https://www.thefreedictionary.com/justice

Larken Rose

An article, published Feb 11, 2022, on his website: (https://www.larkenrose.com/)

Magna Carta, Chapter 39

https://magnacarta.cmp.uea.ac.uk/read/magna_carta_1215/Clause_39

Common Law

https://www.thefreedictionary.com/common+law

Civil Law

https://www.thefreedictionary.com/civil

Ecclesiastical Law

https://www.thefreedictionary.com/ecclesiastical

Statute Law

https://www.thefreedictionary.com/statute

The Supreme Court Decision from 1992

The Grand Jury Belongs to The People — Antonin Scalia (1992) https://stateofthenation2012.com/?p=36330

Jurors Instruction

Wikipedia: (https://en.wikipedia.org/wiki/Jurors_oath)

Lysander Spooner

An Essay on the Trial by Jury. https://theanarchistlibrary.org/library/lysander-spooner-an-essay-on-the-trial-by-jury#toc1

John H. Langbein

Plea Bargain. https://en.wikipedia.org/wiki/Plea_bargain

Prison Population

- https://nap.nationalacademies.org/catalog/18613/the-growth-of-incarceration-in-the-united-states-exploring-causes
- https://worldpopulationreview.com/country-rankings/incarceration-rates-by-country

Equal Justice USA

website: https://ejusa.org

Restorative Justice Organizations:

- National Association of Community and Restorative Justice: https://www.nacrj.org/
- Restorative Justice Exchange: https://restorativejustice.org/
- Equal Justice USA https://ejusa.org.

Heart of the Matter

https://restorativejustice.org/why-restorative-justice/the-issue/

Reconciliation Over A Life Sentence

https://www.themarshallproject.org/2023/09/16/north-carolina-murder-restorative-justice-donald-fields

See also:

https://why-me.org/ambassadors/ and

https://restorativejustice.org/stories/

USA Review of Dan Pink's book

Drive: The Surprising Truth About What Motivates Us in USA Today: https://usatoday30.usatoday.com/money/books/reviews/2010-01-25-drive25_ST_N.htm

Purpose Economy

https://www.tbd.community/en/a/why-rise-purpose-economy-will-change-how-we-work-forever

Alexander del Mar

The History of Money in America from the Earliest Times to the Establishment of the Constitution

https://www.forgottenbooks.com/en/readbook/TheHistoryof MoneyinAmerica_10620093#121

Declaration of Independence

https://www.archives.gov/founding-docs/declaration-transcript

List of Grievances

https://declaration.fas.harvard.edu/resources/text

List of Signers

https://www.archives.gov/files/founding-docs/declaration-signers-gallery-facts.pdf

Preamble to the Massachusetts Constitution

https://malegislature.gov/Laws/Constitution#preamble

The Bill of Rights

https://www.archives.gov/founding-docs/bill-of-rights-transcript

Maritime Law or Admiralty Law

A field of law relating to, and arising from, the practice of the admiralty courts (tribunals that exercise jurisdiction over all contracts, torts, offenses, or injuries within maritime law) that regulates and settles special problems associated with sea navigation and commerce.

https://legal-dictionary.thefreedictionary.com/Admiralty+and+Maritime+Law

Uniform Commercial Code.

https://www.law.cornell.edu/ucc

Article 3

https://www.investopedia.com/terms/u/uniform-commercial-code.asp

3-104. Negotiable Instrument

https://www.law.cornell.edu/ucc/3/3-104

Summary of Article 3, Uniform Law Commission

https://www.uniformlaws.org/committees/community-home?CommunityKey=3de47325-e364-4bb8-a3e8-44b6be55a58b

Person

Definition of person pursuant to the UCC. https://www.law.cornell.edu/ucc/1/1-201

Consideration

https://www.law.cornell.edu/wex/consideration

Maxims of Law

The maxims of law are a distillation of the thinking over hundreds of years of the Common Law. The intent is to help everyone involved in justice to come to the same conclusion in similar cases so that there is reasonable consistency in how crimes are adjudicated and decided.

From Google: "A maxim is a concise statement of a general principle of law that is used as a guiding truth by judges and lawyers. Maxims are more general than ordinary rules of law, and they formulate a legal policy or ideal. Maxims are not usually considered to be law themselves, but they are applied in deciding cases."

- https://www.britannica.com/topic/legal-maxim
- https://thelegalquorum.com/a-compendium-of-legal-maxims/
- https://kirkslawcorner.com/wp-content/uploads/2020/10/A Collection of Legal Maxims in Law and.pdf
- There is a list of Maxims of Law on the Massachusetts Republic website that the Unity Team maintains http://massachusettsrepublic.org

Maxims of Equity

The Maxims of Equity are needed to mitigate any injustices that are caused by the operation of precedent in Common Law.

- https://www.wikiwand.com/en/Maxims_of_equity
- https://bscholarly.com/maxims-of-equity/
- https://en.wikipedia.org/wiki/Maxims_of_equity

Marrianne Williamson

https://marianne2024.com/

Étienne de La Boétie

https://en.wikipedia.org/wiki/%C3%89tienne_de_La_Bo%C3%A9tie

Discourse on Voluntary Servitude

https://en.wikipedia.org/wiki/Discourse_on_Voluntary_Servitude

Etienne de la Boetie2

https://substack.com/@artofliberty

"Government" - The Biggest Scam in History... Exposed!"

https://government-scam.com/store

Ward Republic

https://en.wikipedia.org/wiki/Ward_republic#cite_ref-polWri_3-0

Sociocracy

- https://en.wikipedia.org/wiki/Sociocracy
- https://www.sociocracyforall.org/sociocracy/

Sociocracy for All

https://SociocracyforAll.org

FOUR

Community

"There is no power for change greater than a community discovering what it cares about."

— Margaret J. Wheatley

"I am of the opinion that my life belongs to the whole community and as long as I live, it is my privilege to do for it whatever I can. I want to be thoroughly used up when I die, for the harder I work the more I live."

— George Bernard Shaw

The etymology of the word community can give us a clue about the significance of community. It has its roots in Latin and is made up of **co** which can be used with many words such as co-trustee or co-conspirator or co-operator, etc. to mean *together with,* and **munus** which means *service, gift, duty, offering, tribute, or office.* So community indicates our together service, gifts, offerings, tributes, or offices. This understanding of the meaning of community is significant because it leads us to see that our community is made up of our service to each other, the gifts we offer each other, the tribute we accord each other, and the offices we occupy together. Community is not about imposing norms, or rules and regulations, or government, it is about what the individual member of the community desires to offer as a service and gift, who they desire to honor, and with whom they desire to work.

Community is a natural law phenomenon. We are born into a nuclear family, which is part of an extended family (grandparents, uncles, aunts, cousins, etc.), which is part of a clan (that also includes their relations), which is part of a tribe that shares a culture, traditions, language, religion, etc., which is part of a social compact (jurisdiction) where they are located, a village, town, or city, which is part of a County, a State, and Nation, which has its place in the world. We live in one world nowadays. What we buy comes from all over the world. We are global citizens. But it has come at a price: the multinational companies and the World Trade Organisation (WTO) 'governing' the world economy today have eviscerated our local communities.

The powers-that-ought-not-to-be have created social conditions, with their debt and wage slavery, that have broken up and scattered all the communities to which we would naturally belong, even the nuclear family. It could even be argued that they are working on confusing our children about whether they belong to the sisterhood of women or the brotherhood of men. Although most of us still have a feeling for family, the next level of community promoted by the Official Story is our political leanings (Democrat or Republican) and our Nation. If one identifies as an Independent, a Libertarian, or a Green and feels no allegiance or patriotism towards the American Empire, one will not find oneself reflected in the Official Story.

I am a Green Libertarian because both the Greens and Libertarians include dethroning the banking cartel in their political platforms, and I am dedicated to obviating the American Empire. I do not figure in the Official Story, except as someone who bears watching because I am not consenting to government overreach and propaganda.

The community we may feel the most allegiance to is the artificial community created by our employment. Spending hours with our co-workers creates camaraderie. Often we share parts of our lives with our co-workers, we socialize with them, attend functions together, invite them into our homes, become friends, etc. Our participation in that community typically ends when we retire, are laid off or fired, or quit.

Cooperative businesses offer a more substantial community because the stakeholders are all involved in the management. The <u>Mondragon Cooperatives</u> is in 44 Countries. It is an example of what is possible when the workers are also capitalists and the capitalists are workers. The sense of community in the Mondragon Cooperatives is substantial. The <u>Evergreen Cooperatives</u> in Cleveland are emulating Mondragon Even with a debt based monetary system, it is possible to create a community, grassroots, bottom up economy. This is because cooperatives recognize that the workers must also be capitalists to participate worthily in their destinies.

Many of us have very little in common with our neighbors, even if we live in a small town. We simply do not experience much community where we live. When I was in college, I took a course called "Urban Planning". When I asked the question, "Why are cities designed so that we do not know our neighbors, even though we live so close together?" the class erupted in agreement - they had the same question - but the Professor had no reasonable answer. He pointed out that he had to present the material in the syllabus and we had to learn it if we wanted to pass the course. That experience and others, in the Spring of 1969, led me to conclude that a college education is designed to indurate us to a profoundly sick society.

> *"It is no measure of health to be well adjusted to a profoundly sick society."*
>
> - Krishnamurti

The thing that can create community in this day and age is a spiritually inspired common ideal. If I desire to be in a community where my service and gifts are recognized and appreciated, it will be by volunteering for an idealistic social service organization or a New England-style town committee. Belonging to a congregation in a church may satisfy my natural longing for community, and if the church could issue money, it would be in a position to change the circumstances of my life. It could become a Jural Assembly.

Wouldn't it be great to belong to a community that recognizes who we are and appreciates and funds the service(s) we choose to offer our community? Wouldn't it be great to grow up in a community where we are expected to discover our life calling and be supported financially in developing our skills to serve that life calling? Wouldn't it be great to belong to a community where we participate in discovering what is true, in creating something beautiful, and in dedicating ourselves to "doing the good"?

The ideas or perspectives we need to create a better world center around the arrangements and agreements we make to satisfy our needs and desires. Let us assume that we belong to a Jural Assembly where justice is based on the Golden Rule and Do No Harm and our only commitment to that social compact is to show up when selected to serve on a Jury. Let us further assume that our Jural Assembly understands the sovereign issues the currency to create the circumstances of our lives, and we all commit to active consent governance. What follows is an imaginary musing about what life could be like in such a society to provide understanding, clarity, and inspiration about what is possible.

Musings

> Ah ... Thank you for asking me to tell you a little about my experience in my Jural Assembly Community. Growing up in my Jural Assembly Community, I knew when I reached

my majority that the question I would be answering was, "What need or desire do I see that I would like to participate in satisfying?"

I aspired to be an artist. I was drawn to making what I call sculpture-paintings. I sometimes made the sculpture part out of clay and sometimes I carved them out of wood. Since I often had a hard time holding them to work on them, I sketched a type of vise that I thought would solve the problem and that I could possibly make. I wondered if someone was already making something similar and if my sketch was significantly different. I asked the organizations that were making a similar tool if they might be interested in pursuing my idea. If so, I would join their organization (typically a multi-stakeholder cooperative).

When I talked to the Widget Cooperative, they considered my idea and asked me to determine how much capital I would be responsible for to implement the idea. Since I am not a businessman and did not know how to make a business plan or determine how much capital I needed, I went to the Business Plan Circle in my Jural Assembly Community. I described to the Business Plan Circle what I desired to do and that the Widget Co-operative is willing to consider adding my vise to their product line. The Business Plan Circle offered me a choice of people with whom to consult to come up with the needed business plan. After reviewing their resumes and doing some interviews, I chose Peter Planner.

Peter Planner first wanted to know what experiences the inspiration for the idea came from so that we may know with whom to speak about its utility. He explained we should not make any assumptions about how well my vise would solve my and other artists' problems. We need to make our assumptions explicit. We decided that we needed a prototype. With Peter Planner's help, I found a company that specializes in making prototypes. They gave me a price that Peter Planner thought was reasonable. So I went online to my bank account and typed the amount into my bank account. Then I transferred those funds to the prototype company.

I was very pleased with the widget prototype; it works well for what I need. Unfortunately, after showing it to 50 businesses, and to many artists that I thought would like it, only one artist was willing to buy one at an unrealistically low price. Peter Planner and I agreed while the prototype was useful to me, it was not the basis for an addition to the Widget Co-operative's product line. Since I am responsible for the value of the prototype, I asked the Banking Circle if what the prototype cost might cause some inflation because the value was not realized. The Banker with whom I spoke said I should treat it as a purchase, not as an investment, and reduce my consumption over a year or two to account for that lower than expected value. I divided the cost of the prototype by 24 and instructed the bank to reduce my community dividend by that amount for each of the next 24 months.

Widget Cooperative impressed me as an organization and since I am an artist and designer, I asked their Inventors Circle if I might join them in making their products more beautiful. They agreed. To see what I could do, they asked me to beautify a specific product nearing the end of its production life cycle. This was very exciting to me; I felt recognized and encouraged. After studying the product for a while, I decided to just change the proportions of the handle and head. I made the handle a little longer and the head a bit broader so they followed the proportions of the Golden Ratio. I also added some pale neutral, but complementary, colors to the handle and head. I showed my design at the next meeting of the Inventors Circle and they agreed it was more pleasing to the eye. When I explained what I had done, they became enthusiastic about the potential of the

Golden Ratio being applied more generally. They recommended me to the Onboarding Circle as my next step in becoming involved with the Cooperative.

The Onboarding Circle checked me out and a few days later they gave me homework to learn the history and the culture of the Widget Cooperative. They said if I felt that I was in alignment with their culture and aim, I could propose how I would participate in the Widget Cooperative. They accepted my proposal of spending a few days every month improving the designs for their products. They told me how much capital I would need to invest and what percentage of the dividend I could expect. I wrote the amount of the capital investment into my bank account and transferred it to their capital account. I wasn't clear how I should account for the dividend from the Widget Cooperative, relative to the reduction in my Community Dividend (because I would now be using my prototype at least once a month). I talked to the Banking Circle and followed their recommendation.

After six months, I was working four or five days a month with the Widget Cooperative with the design team I had assembled. In addition to making the products more beautiful to look at, we were redesigning production machinery to make it more flexible and robust (less maintenance and downtime). The profits from the increased demand for the more beautiful widgets were funding the machinery improvements. After about a year, the design team formed its own co-op, The Golden Ratio Design Coop, and offered its services to all the companies within a day's drive from the Widget Coop. The Business Plan Circle and Peter Planner were a big help in getting things organized, and coordinated with the New Business Circle of the Jural Assembly Bank. Currently my monthly dividend is much higher than it had been.

While keeping my commitment to no more than 5 days a month, I created a free lending art gallery for my more whimsical and purely artistic sculpture paintings. I issued the capital needed to set up the gallery and make it beautiful in consultation with the Arts Council and the people who had bought my artwork in the past. I am now offering to include other artists' work in my Gallery, and the idea of borrowing art like a book is meeting with enthusiasm.

Every month, I attend an Economic Health meeting for my Ward, where we learn how well we are doing, what the Community Dividend is likely to be over the next few months, and what the economic prospects are for our Jural Assembly, our County, and State. We also evaluate the numbers on our community balance sheet to improve our economic health. The number we are working on is to bring down the cost of the Emergency Room as a percentage of the overall cost of the Hospital. The assumption is that overuse of the Emergency Room indicates a failure of the healthcare system generally or of the people not doing preventive care.

Recently, I attended a trial to adjudicate a dispute between a community group that damned up a stream that had once been dammed a long time ago and an environmental group that tore it down. Each group had accused the other of causing harm. The Grand Jury determined that both groups had probable cause and issued a Presentment to both groups with instructions to prepare for a Trial by Jury. At the trial, each group presented its case to the Jury. The Community Group argued that the fishing pond and swimming hole created by the dam was of greater value to the neighborhood than any minimal environmental damage it might cause. The Environmental Group cited the history that the original dam had been removed to protect the unique species of swamp grass and a salamander that lived only there. I was sympathetic to both arguments, so I was pleased with the Jury's verdict. Namely, the Community Group could build the dam but only if its plan preserved the habitat of the salamander and swamp grass in a way that was agreeable to the Environmental Group. The Facilitator of our Ward, who is widely acknowledged to be among the best facilitators in our Jural Assembly, was selected by the Jury to mediate the effort. The final solution was not to build a dam. Instead, the Community Group would deepen a portion of the stream that could be used for fishing and swimming, and which would leave the swamp intact.

I would love to be called for Jury Duty, but I understand that it is unlikely since there is so little call for adjudicating harm.

There is much more to tell about how my life has developed, but let me just say that when I heard the phrase: "The Community is as it should be and I am doing my utmost to make it so!" I said, "Yes, that is so true!"

We, the People, need a Community in which we may discover what we are interested in, what we see needs to be done, and even what we desire to dedicate our lives to accomplish. We, the People, need a Community in which our service and gifts are recognized and appreciated. We do not need a community or a government to tell us what to do or compel us to fulfill someone else's vision. May the world be as We, the People, dream it to be!

Economics in Community

The Free, sovereign individual, living in a Just society and a collaborative Community will experience that competition is necessary only to determine the best of something, and that collaboration is necessary to manifest it. In the world our heart knows is possible, individuals are at liberty to act out of their inspiration to generate ideas to "make the world a better place". Implementing good ideas requires people to collaborate to influence hearts and minds and/or transform nature into a useful product. This image of individual inspiration and community collaboration is what we need to understand economics. Consider for a moment that nearly everything we need and desire is provided to us by other people doing something that we value. The question to answer is: "How would we organize the economy if it were up to us"?

The social science known as 'Economics' is called the dismal science because an inescapable element of 'economics' is human misery. The banking cartel promotes the ideology of 'Economics' because one of its foundational tenets is that money and banking are only neutral intermediaries between savers and borrowers. If the banks were neutral intermediaries, they would not be able to influence the economy. However, as you may remember from Chapter One, nothing could be further from the truth. What 'Economics' calls the business cycle (booms and busts) are purely financial phenomena intentionally engineered by the banking system. Banks create booms by lowering interest rates and relaxing lending criteria. They create busts by raising interest rates and tightening lending criteria. Banks conjure the money they lend, but 'Economics' claims that money is a commodity that can be bought and sold in the market, that its value depends on its scarcity, and the price of money is the cost of borrowing.

Collateral for a huge portion of bank debt is commercial and residential property. It is the increase in the value of land that creates the differential between good and bad neighborhoods, so 'Economics' treats land as a commodity and redlines the poor neighborhoods. Since the cost of labor (human resources) is a major expense, labor is also considered a commodity. Taxes and political speech (campaign money) are necessary expenses(i.e. a cost of doing business) to maintain the infrastructure and the political climate so that the businesses that make up the economy can continue to thrive. The cost of doing business for the dominant corporations includes capturing the regulatory agencies that were originally tasked with protecting the public. Lately, 'Economics' has been maintaining that the National Debt is not a significant factor in the economy.

The other tenet of the 'Economics' profession that flies in the face of our experience is that people are primarily motivated by their self-interest, security, and acquisition of material goods. In other words, 'Economics' treats us as though we were only fearful and greedy. Since we know that this is not true, we need a new social science of economics that will give us the ideas and practices so everyone may collaborate productively in creating the kind of economy they believe will serve Justice and Freedom.

The premise of a true science of economics is that everyone is primarily motivated by their desire to recognize and fulfill their life's purpose, what they feel inspired to dedicate their life to. This means that issuing money and regulating the money supply must serve the people to facilitate their efforts to self-actualize. People motivated by their transcendent purpose are not a commodity to be exploited. Likewise, land - in the sense of Nature and the environment - is also not a commodity to be exploited. Money is also not a commodity that can be bought and sold. When money or capital cannot be bought or sold, but is a right, then doing things 'for the money' ceases. Instead we do things because they need to be done to satisfy the needs and desires of the community. This is an aspect of our life purpose and our self-actualization.

When we recognize Land (nature), Labor (people), and Capital (money) as the Commons, we will remove them from the economy and place them squarely in the province of governance and culture. We will then have a straightforward basis for understanding Production, Distribution, and Consumption. This is the true province of economics. The purpose of production and distribution is consumption. What is required for efficient and sustainable production? What is required for equitable and sustainable distribution? What is the responsibility of the consumer? These are the questions to address when we develop a true social science of economics.

A collaborative economy will support our desire for a just and sustainable abundance.

"...The people can and will be furnished with a currency as safe as their own Government. Money will cease to be master and become the servant of humanity. Democracy will rise superior to the money power."

- <u>Abraham Lincoln</u>, address to Congress in 1865.

Developing a True Social Science of Economics

Developing a new understanding of economics involves a few key insights.

1. Money is an agreement or law to use something to measure value and to facilitate transparent value-for-value trades. Money is not a thing, it is not valuable in itself. Money *measures* value. The decisions on what to issue money for are a function of governance, not economics.
2. The purpose of production is not to "make money", it is consumption. Consumers need to take responsibility for what is produced.
3. Nature (and the services provided by nature), People (and the work they do), and Money (including the credit needed for the means of production) are not commodities to be bought and sold. They are the Commons for which we are all responsible.
4. Only those useful material objects, goods, and services, that have an existence independent of the people producing them, have a measurable value. Everything dependent on the capacities of individuals has unmeasurable value.
5. The unmeasurable values are spirit manifesting. Spirit manifesting is supported by the means of production and the

infrastructure, all of which are made up of measurable values. The unmeasurable values are the domain of governance and culture.

6. There is a true or objective price for everything that is produced and it increases as the item moves from raw material and production through distribution to consumption. The true price assures that all the costs, including the environmental (nature), social costs (governance), and cultural (science, art, and education/religion/spirituality), are included in the price.

These understandings are described in detail below.

Money Measures Value

Firstly, money is what we need to *measure value*. A measure is established by custom, agreement, or by law. The measuring tool is designed to be accurate. Money is no different. The unit of value ought to be something that everyone can relate to, so they have a sense of what it is worth. Historically, the most common measures of value have been a bushel of wheat, the Shekel, and an ounce of gold or silver. A <u>troy ounce of gold</u> is the weight of 480 grains of wheat or barley kernels from the center of the stalk. We are so removed from agriculture that hardly any of us would have a visceral sense for what a bushel of wheat is worth. We do have a visceral sense for an hour of our labor. So the unit of value could be set as an hour of unskilled labor, for example, an hour of moving and stacking firewood, or an hour of filling bags with sand for flood control, etc. We also have a sense for the importance of, if not the value of, electricity, so we might use a Kilowatt hour as the unit of value. Or perhaps there may be a much better basis for the unit of value we may more easily agree to. We can, of course, continue to use the dollar, since that is what we are used to, and fix it so it no longer inflates.

The *means of exchange* is the device we use to make the unit of value useful in making value-for-value trades. The means of exchange is half of the bargain, it measures the value of something sold in the past so it can be the other half of the bargain when buying something now. It can be coins or notes (cash) or a ledger system, or just transfers in bank accounts.

The unit of measure is an agreement or law, and the regulation of the measuring device is a governance task. Units of measure and measuring devices are part of the infrastructure for the economy and our prosperity. *"Congress shall have power ... to coin money and regulate the value thereof and of foreign coin and fix the standard of weights and measures."*

To make this clearer, the analogy of time is useful. The unit of value is a unit of time. The means of exchange is the measuring tool used to measure the passage of time.

Wikipedia defines a <u>unit of time</u> as any particular time interval, used as a standard way of measuring or expressing duration. Historically, many units of time were defined by the movements of astronomical objects, such as the sun, the moon, and the earth (e.g. a day is the time for a complete earth rotation).

We have invented many devices to measure the passage of time. These tools are analogous to the means of exchange for money. Just like it has taken a while to perfect the clock, it will take some time to perfect the measuring instrument or the means of exchange.

- A sundial uses a <u>gnomon</u> to cast a shadow on a set of markings calibrated to the hour and the shadow marks the hour in local time.
- A <u>water clock</u> was one of the most precise timekeeping devices in ancient Egypt which measured the flow of liquid into or out of a vessel, and where the amount of liquid can then be measured.

- Fire clocks, such as a notched candle or the Chinese practice of burning a knotted rope, measured time in the absence of sunlight. All fire clocks were of a measured size to approximate the passage of time, noting the length of time required for fire to travel from one knot to the next.
- The <u>hourglass</u> uses the flow of sand to measure the flow of time and was used in navigation.
- The pendulum clock became popular in the 1600s when Dutch astronomer <u>Christiaan Huygens</u> applied the pendulum and balance wheel to regulate the movement of clocks.
- Quartz-crystal clocks were invented in the 1930s, improving timekeeping performance far beyond that of pendulums.
- The most accurate timekeeping devices are <u>atomic clocks</u>, which are accurate to seconds in many millions of years and are used to calibrate other clocks and timekeeping instruments.

Just to make this analogy crystal clear, Time and Value both need to be measured. We measure time in years, months, weeks, and days, and the instrument is a calendar. We measure time in hours, minutes, and seconds, and the instrument is a watch or clock. We do not believe that having a clock gives us extra hours (although our experience of time can be fast or slow as in "time flies" or "it's about time"). We measure value with money. While our experience of the relative value of things is also variable, we use the same word for both the measure and the instrument, namely "money". This is the source of confusion. Society is engineered so that we will believe that money is a valuable thing or is valuable unto itself, which, if it is truly money, it is not.

We propose that *the unit of value* be called the **Juno** and *the measuring instrument, (i.e. the means of exchange),* be called **Moneta**. These names come from <u>Juno Moneta</u>, the Roman Queen of the Gods, the protector of marriage, and the embodiment of the feminine and abundance. The Roman mint was in her temple on Capitoline Hill.

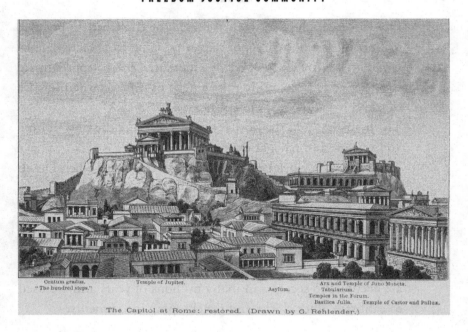

Centum gradus.
"The hundred steps."   Temple of Jupiter.   Arx and Temple of Juno Moneta.
                                        Asylum.   Tabularium.
                                   Temples in the Forum.
                                   Basilica Julia.   Temple of Castor and Polluz.
The Capitol at Rome: restored. (Drawn by G. Rehlender.)

Throughout our history, we have had an inflating or deflating measure of value. It may take us a while to learn how to keep the Juno as an accurate measure of value by learning to regulate Moneta so there is always the right amount circulating. Three things must be kept in balance:

- The amount of Moneta circulating (Money Stock),
- the Velocity at which the Moneta circulates (how many trades Moneta is facilitating in, say, a month), and
- The amount of Moneta not circulating because it is being saved (Savings Rate).

If the circulation speeds up, there may be too much Moneta in circulation. If the circulation slows down, there may not be enough Monteta in circulation. Moneta will need to be subtracted from or added to circulation. If the savings rate increases, more Moneta might need to be issued, and if the savings rate decreases, some Moneta may need to be removed from circulation. In this way, the Juno will neither inflate or deflate but maintain its utility as an accurate measure of value.

This would obviate the need for any calculations about net present value or internal rate of return, etc. which are all distortions resulting from interest and inflation.

Purpose of Production is Consumption

Secondly, a "free market" is a misnomer since the market is currently created and regulated by the laws, rules, and regulations governing commerce. The monopolistic pharmaceutical and food companies have captured the regulatory agencies that were established to protect the consumers so they may lie to us and sell medicines and food that create the obesity, diabetes, alzheimer, autism and cancer epidemics. 'Economics' promotes the "free market" to perpetuate the idea that consumers freely choose what they desire based on the advertising and marketing information available to them. Why does the advertising and marketing information not talk about how addictive sugar is, why is it added to just about everything? Why do we not know that rats choose sugar over cocaine? Why do we not know that mammals never choose to eat GMO grains if they have a choice of real grains?

Most efforts to persuade consumers to act responsibly to undo the harm done by global companies are grassroots, underfunded, nonprofits. These organizations are exposing the harms being done to our bodies and our planet and are seeking to remedy them with lawsuits, boycotts, etc. What if consumers always participated in determining what would be produced? Is "voting with our dollars" really enough? What if everything that gets produced had to go through the healthy collective judgment of an active-consent-based group of organized consumers? What if the efficacy of the product for the intended purpose always had an appropriate timetable for when it would be evaluated? What if the information about a product were simply factual? What if the role of the distributor included mediating the interests of the producers and the consumers? I am so looking forward to delving into these questions with a conscious group of consumers!

Nature, People, and Money

Thirdly, the existing Economy has commodified Nature, People, and Money to serve the interests of the hidden sovereign, the powers-that-not-ought-to-be.

Nature provides myriad services to support our life, from our bodies to the soil, food, medicines, water, and air, to the forces we do not normally see. People create all the material values we trade by transforming nature into useful goods and services. Money makes the goods and services in the economy commensurate so that we may compare their values and determine what trades of value-for-value would serve us and make us better off.

If we recognize that Nature, People, and Money are not commodities, but are what constitute the Commons, then we will make arrangements for production, distribution, and consumption that does not harm nature, does not denigrate people, and neutralizes the power of money (i.e. restricting it to the measure of value (Juno) and means of exchange (Moneta). Unlike Nature and People, money is a social convention, something that we create to serve our purposes. Nature, people, and money must never be bought or sold!

Measurable Value

Fourthly, only those useful material objects, goods, and services that have their existence separate from the people who produce them have measurable value. We, as consumers, are perfectly happy to pay the stated price if we have confidence that it was arrived at objectively. We may choose what level of quality or utility we want to pay for. We are willing to pay more for organic or out of season strawberries, etc. The farmers selling their produce at the farmers market need to include all their costs, including their living expenses, tractors and machinery, greenhouses, seeds or seedlings, compost, and what we normally think of as taxes and charitable giving, in the price attributable to each of their crops.

This is true of all the things in the economy. Raw materials to finished goods move through the economy from production, to distribution, to consumption based on their price. Each stage of production and distribution sets the price of the item to represent the share of the entire cost attributable to each stage. The price of a car when it leaves the factory is set by the people producing it to cover the entire cost of producing it, or the <u>cost of goods sold</u>. Currently, these costs fall into the general sub-categories of direct labor, direct materials, and overhead. Direct labor and direct materials are variable costs, while overhead consists of fixed costs (such as utilities, rent, and supervisory salaries). As the car moves through the distribution system and is finally sold to the consumer, additional costs of shipping, advertising, marketing, accounting, research and development, litigation, travel, meals, management salaries, bonuses, taxes, and profit are added to the price of the car. External costs are not included. These include the costs of the infrastructure, health and environmental damages, and recycling or disposal. These costs are borne by We, the People.

In the society to benefit everyone, the true price will include the living expenses of the people producing it as a dividend and not just the wages or salaries. All of the direct material costs are included as are the fixed costs of the factory. So too are all of the currently externalized costs included in the true price: infrastructure, mitigating any health and environmental damages (if they exist), the entire lifecycle of the product (repurposing, recycling, disposal), the cost of justice and the cost of the culture that supports the well being of the people making it. The retailer pays the factory the stated true price and sells the car to the consumer for a price that includes all the costs of the retailer, including the living expenses of the people, the infrastructure, the social and cultural costs, etc. These costs are all calculable because the thing priced has its existence separate from the people who produced it. The price of the repaired car, or the cleaned rug, or the installed furnace, etc. also includes all those costs.

The price must not be too low because it excludes costs (e.g. such things as the cost of disposal or recycling, or damage to the environment, etc.), or too high because it includes unjust enrichment. When the item has a true price, then the demand for value-for-value in each exchange will reveal the true worth of the product at the point at which it is consumed.

The existing economy maintains that prices are set by the market as a result of supply and demand. Supply is one of those false ideas that is so popular. There is only demand, the demand for value. In the new understanding of economics, We, the People, issue money to measure the values produced. We provide a record, or accounting, of those values as the basis for making judgments about their value. Both parties to the exchange demand (require) value. The good or service is one value and the money is the other value as a placeholder representing the value of a previous good or service. We could say the money is half the bargain. See E.C. Riegel, which is important for understanding that the true price is not a function of a "free market, supply and demand".

All measurable, economic, material things from raw materials to finished goods, in the context of the prevailing culture and social order, arise as a result of intelligent human labor. If the unit of value, the Juno, is set as an hour of unskilled labor or some other easily felt value, then it becomes possible to establish a price for everything that includes the cost of the goods and services needed for our governance and for our culture. When we are clear that nature, people, and money are not things with a price, then it becomes possible to come up with an objective price for material goods and services.

Unmeasurable Value

Fifthly, our distaste for money has its origins in the prevailing culture which assumes it can put a price on everything, including the life and worth of a human being, the natural world, and our governments. Things of immeasurable value are simply things which can not be measured or have a price tag hung on them. It signifies the absence of a quantifiable attribute or quality. Everything solely dependent on the services rendered by individuals has unmeasurable value. What is the value of the inspiring teacher? The nurturing mother? The severely disabled person requiring continuous care? The skillful hands of a surgeon?

The infrastructure needed for the people to create unmeasurable value contains the things that have measurable value, such as the house, the car, the labor-saving devices, the healthy, sustainably grown food, the tools, etc. We desire to have all the things that make it possible for us to devote ourselves to the transcendent purpose we feel called to serve that creates unmeasurable value. It is the creation of the unmeasurable value that is motivating.

The beauty of something is also unmeasurable. This beauty can either be natural or manmade. What is the value of a colorful landscape? The flowing lines of a sculpture? The pleasantness of public spaces? The feeling of peace in a building?

The house, the car, the washing machine, the public spaces, and even the roads should be true, beautiful, and good. They should be true to their purpose, inspirationally beautiful, and manifestly good. Waldorf Education is well aware of the need for the school environment to be beautiful, and for the faculty to be true to their mission and always focused on doing the good. Modern architecture, in contrast, is often ugly, not well suited to its purpose, and environmentally destructive, but cheap. See Waldorf Architecture or Camphill for some examples.

Emotions, (love, happiness, security) and intangible concepts (justice, freedom, self-determination) are unmeasurable since they cannot be precisely quantified or expressed in numerical terms. What is the value of a community that feels happy and secure? What is the value of justice? Of equitable distribution? Of good governance? The spirit of a justly governed, collaborative, sustainable community?

Expressing our life's purpose is supported by production and the infrastructure, all of which are made up of measurable values. The unmeasurable values are the domain of governance and culture.

True Price

Sixthly is the importance of the true price. The true price includes the costs of repurposing, recycling, disposal, and the costs of governing and the culture, etc. The consumers, for whom the production exists, will be committed to paying the true price if they have confidence that it is objective. Eighty four percent of consumers say they will not buy from a company that has a poor environmental record and 55% will pay more for eco-friendly brands. Since it is largely price competition that is the rationale for externalizing costs there will be no incentive to do that if consumers were to form consumer associations and become involved in the pricing of the goods in demand. Consumers would not agree to export production to China, or anywhere else, to take advantage of cheap labor. Once we commit to paying the true price, and participating in assuring justice, we will grasp that we have no desire to sell our labor. We will acutely experience the immorality of anyone having to work a crappy job because they need the money to live. And we will be pleased that everyone has an appropriate dividend income and everything that we do on our own or together is a voluntary initiative. We, the People, will desire that our understanding of money and unmeasurable value, issuing money, and governing by consent would be spread worldwide.

The Economic Cycle

Our ability to appreciate the economic cycle, from inspiration through production to consumption in a way that supports the governance and culture necessary to inspire new production, profoundly impacts our understanding of Community.

The entrepreneur embodies this process. The value of the enterprise results from the entrepreneur's inspiration and competence. The resulting value supports the entire context from which it arose. This is the process we need to make the basis of economics.

The entrepreneur lives in a cultural context which allows an inspiration to manifest. The idea is inspired by the desire to make the world a better place and not to "make money". The idea is realized as the entrepreneur organizes the world to manifest it, either by acquiring the necessary skills or by motivating others with those skills to join them. Then they capitalize the necessary infrastructure to produce the goods or the service. The response to the manifested idea (from sales or donations) satisfies a need or desire in its community. The ongoing value generation contributes to the development of the culture that supports the process happening again. The entrepreneur stands on the shoulders of all the entrepreneurs who went before. In one way or another, we may all be entrepreneurs when our community is oriented to recognizing and furthering our initiatives to make the world a better place.

This understanding allows us to let go of the dismal science and consider how we will create the new story, our story, the one that leads to the society that benefits everyone.

Shall we continue to believe that love of money is the root of all evil? Might we come to believe that love of Juno Moneta is the spirit realized?

What do we need to do to find out? What might we do to manifest this vision?

In the next chapter we look at how we will create the new model for a society based on Freedom, Justice, and Community.

Endnotes

See Just Abundance website for additional information on these topics

- For EndNotes: https://www.justabundance.org/fj
- Appendixes: https://www.justabundance.org/appendixes

Munus

https://www.latin-is-simple.com/en/vocabulary/noun/12419/?h=munus

Mondragon Cooperatives

https://www.mondragon-corporation.com/en/about-us/

Evergreen Cooperatives

Evergreen's Fund for Employee Ownership is a groundbreaking investment fund, designed to create quality jobs through employee ownership while anchoring jobs and wealth in the local community.

https://www.evgoh.com/tfeo

Golden Ratio

https://en.wikipedia.org/wiki/Golden_ratio

Redlining

https://www.bankrate.com/real-estate/what-is-redlining/

Abraham Lincoln

on the subject of Constitutional Money; from an address to Congress in 1865. https://www.goodreads.com/quotes/288057-the-privilege-of-creating-and-issuing-money-is-not-only

Troy Ounce of Gold

https://www.investopedia.com/terms/t/troyounce.asp

Unit Of Time

https://en.wikipedia.org/wiki/Unit_of_time

Gnomon

https://en.wikipedia.org/wiki/Gnomon

Water Clock

https://en.wikipedia.org/wiki/Water_clock

Hourglass

https://en.wikipedia.org/wiki/Hourglass

Christiaan Huygens

https://www.encyclopedia.com/people/science-and-technology/physics-biographies/christiaan-huygens

Atomic Clocks

https://en.wikipedia.org/wiki/Atomic_clock

Juno Moneta

https://en.wikipedia.org/wiki/Temple_of_Juno_Moneta

Cost of Goods Sold

- https://www.accountingtools.com/articles/cost-of-goods-sold
- https://www.investopedia.com/terms/c/cogs.asp
- https://corporatefinanceinstitute.com/resources/accounting/cost-of-goods-sold-cogs/

E.C. Riegel

https://reinventingmoney.com/?s=E.C.+Riegel

Waldorf Architecture

- https://www.archdaily.com/935990/how-to-design-schools-and-interiors-based-on-waldorf-pedagogy
- https://www.waldorftoday.com/2018/06/world-of-waldorf-school-architecture/

Camphill

- https://camphill-schulgemeinschaften.de/standorte/foehrenbuehl/
- https://en.wikipedia.org/wiki/Camphill_Movement

Environmentally conscious consumer statistics

https://theroundup.org/environmentally-conscious-consumer-statistics/

FIVE

Creating The New Model

"You never change things by fighting the existing reality. To change something, build a new model that makes the existing model obsolete."

- Buckminster Fuller

In the Official Story, everything that is credit-worthy gets funded and whatever the banks consider to be of questionable value does not. If what we desire to do will be profitable, it will be funded with loans or investments; if it is not-for-profit, it will be funded with grants or by the Government. The problem with this Official Story is that so much that we would value if we could get funding doesn't get funded. This has given rise to the local investing movement and the various fundraising websites such as kickstarter, indiegogo, patreon and gofundme. The success of local investing and crowdfunding demonstrate the desire of consumers for more participation in deciding what happens.

In this chapter, we describe the bell to ring to gather the group, the meeting protocols, the organizational structure, and the funding mechanism to turn the society that benefits everyone from a utopian idea that is easily dismissed to the new reality. The Cooperative model is particularly well suited to community building and Open Book Management is about understanding the finances of our cooperatives. The goal is to call together a Jural Assembly Community in the sense of the Jeffersonian Ward Republic capable of providing the functions of governance to each other.

The Bell to Ring

This book advocates for the ideas we need to create the world that we know in our hearts we desire. Those concepts are Freedom, Justice, and Community. The world we know in our hearts is made up of **Free** individuals, who actively consent to maintain a **Just** society, and collaborate in a nurturing **Community** to provide everything that we need and desire.

These concepts are what we can use to sound the bell of liberty and encourage people, who are already active and productive, to usher in the new world. We may find better ways to express the idea, so that it may lead the movement to 'shift the paradigm', and guide the deliberations of many groups toward the manifestation of their dreams.

What we do not need to do is try to convince anyone of the rightness of our views, or that our ideas provide the only or even the best solution.

"A mind convinced against its will is of the same mind still."

- Benjamin Franklin

We need to be clear to ourselves that the banking cartel has appropriated human nature for its benefit. If we desire to create something different from current reality, we need to do something that is life-empowering with money.

Group Forming Questions

Nearly everyone we know is aware of the importance of money in their life. Here are some examples of questions that can start a conversation to possibly create a willingness to increase their understanding of money.

1. "Do you know who issues the money, the US Dollar?" Hardly anyone ever gets this question right. However, correcting them does not generally help.

2. "Do you think it would be important to know that?" works better as a follow up question. It is best to leave it at that, and steer the ensuing conversation to getting them to tell you what is important to them, what they have dedicated their life to, or would want to if they didn't have to earn their living doing something they do not love doing.

3. At some point in that conversation, you could ask something along the lines of:

   a. "Is your income adequate so that you are not always stressed by a lack of money and you are able to do what needs to be done?" Or

   b. "If you knew you could have the money to do that, would you want to organize your life to do it? Or

   c. "If you had a blank check you knew you could use to fund it, would you do what you described as your transcendent purpose?

4. The aim is to invite people to answer the question "What does the world you know in your heart you desire look like? Would you like to help create it?"

Maybe there are various groups that you belong to where you could practice beginning the conversation. Of course, asking people to read this book could be helpful as well!

Sociocracy

Hopefully, we will either start a group that aims to create the society that benefits everyone, or join a group that is willing to add it to their agenda. The first step is learning about <u>Sociocracy</u> or dynamic governance. WIkipedia defines sociocracy as:

> Sociocracy is a theory of governance that seeks to create psychologically safe environments and productive organizations. It draws on the use of consent, rather than majority voting, in discussion and decision-making by people who have a shared goal or work process.

Sociocracy has a meeting process and an organizational structure that will aid in developing a well-run Jural Assembly.

The word "sociocracy" is derived from the Latin "socios" (companion) and Greek kratein (to govern). Sociocracy means rule by the "socios", people who have a social relationship with one another, as opposed to democracy, governance by the "demos" or the general mass of people. Socio-cracy is governance by people who know and associate with one another.

Sociocracy arises out of a profound understanding of our social nature. It is the necessary counter to the evils perpetuated by democracy, which disenfranchises up to 49% of a populace through voting. It is relatively easy to propagandize the "demos" since they do not converse with each other, unlike the "socios" who do. The "demos" have been propagandized to accept all the evils rampant in our world (wars, poverty, surveillance, capitalism, etc.) This is perfectly understandable as the powers-that-ought-not-to-be have an endless supply of money to buy the culture (science, art, and spirituality/ religion/ education) and the governance (legislative, executive, and judicial), and to control the economy (production, distribution, and consumption).

We, the People, will organize as the "socios", not the "demos". Our society will be organized sociocratically, in interconnected circles of people who know and associate with each other. By working together in groups (or circles) and meeting regularly, these circles can meet the objective (aim or transcendent purpose) they agreed to accomplish. If we are meeting regularly to create the better world, how easy will it be to propagandize us? Will we love to be truth seekers, beautifiers and do-gooders?

Meeting Protocols

The meeting protocols are the essence of how the "socios" will govern. In a sociocratic meeting, each member is participating in a particular circle or group because the objective of that circle interests them. A society organized to be sociocractic consists of interlocking circles of people committed to accomplishing the aim or objective of their circles.

Each circle is guided by its aim. For example, the circle of people who responded to the bell that was rung will have the initial aim of developing a powerful imagination of the Society that Benefits Everyone. The aim could be phrased as "Imagining Community". If you are convening the group, you will be the leader responsible for keeping the people who join the Imagining Community Circle inspired and working towards that aim. If this circle of people are from a congregation, non-profit group, book club, or some other group that you belong to, they could agree to try the sociocratic meeting protocols.

In a sociocratic meeting, everyone's voice matters as everyone has an important piece of the puzzle that is necessary to accomplish our aim. Everyone must feel that they have the opportunity to weigh in on the discussion. This means that we conduct the meeting in "rounds". Each time we go around the circle and hear from each person is called a "round".

At the beginning of the meeting, we agree upon the agenda in the first round. Each item on the agenda is then discussed in a round or series of rounds in which everyone is heard from each time. At the end of the meeting, we evaluate the meeting in a round in which we hear what each one felt about how the meeting was conducted.

This kind of meeting is very satisfying, but can also be very frustrating. Therefore, it needs to be well facilitated. The Facilitator is a role that a member of the group may be selected to take on. The group also needs to select someone responsible for recording the proceedings of the circle and who will make sure that everyone in the circle has access to that information. That person can choose the name for their role, such as Scribe or Administrator. We also need someone to represent the group in the wider context called the Delegate. The Delegate, along with the Leader, will assure that the other groups who are working on the better world are aware of each other and benefit from hearing about each other's work.

The selection process for the roles in a group is an essential element of a sociocratic meeting. It is not a popularity contest. There is no campaigning and no voting. We desire to select the best person for each role. So we hear from each person in a round who they think would be the best person to lead, to facilitate, to administer, to represent. What is so wonderful about this process is that it is full of appreciation for the people in the circle. For example, we are choosing the administrator. Each of us is asked who we think would make the best administrator and why. The "why" is a statement of our appreciation of the person based on our experience of them. After we have heard from each person, it is usually pretty clear who would make a good administrator because the circle will have heard a fair amount about each person nominated. The next round would be the opportunity to change one's nomination and at the end of that round, the facilitator will make a proposal based on their sense of who would be best administrator and will include the terms and evaluation criteria in the proposal. The next round is a consent round. Here's an example of a proposal: "Do you consent to this person being the administrator for the next 6 meetings and on the 7th meeting, we evaluate their performance according to, for example, how long it took us to approve the minutes of the previous meeting." We go around the circle and each person says something to indicate their consent or objection, such as "YES", or "Good Enough for Now," or "Safe Enough to Try", or "I dunno, but ok!" Any objection stops the consent process until it has been resolved. Objections are often about the unintended consequences and usually can be taken care of by shortening or lengthening the term and/or changing the evaluation criteria.

In a sociocratic meeting, every proposal requires consent. Objections must be expressed as a reasoned argument that addresses how the objection interferes with the circle's aim. "I don't like it" is not a good enough argument. We all agree to accept help in expressing the "I don't like it" in a reasoned argument, so the objection can be addressed and the proposal made better.

Every proposal that arises out of our Imagining Community Circle will be to further the aim, either of the imagination itself or how to implement it. Every proposal will be consented to by everyone in the circle as to whether it will further our aim or not. This is the key to understanding the power of sociocracy. Everything passes through the healthy human judgment of a group of people who have come together to accomplish an aim they agree is true, or beautiful or good or maybe all three.

Consent

The consent round is the way a sociocratic meeting and organization creates the conditions in which everything that happens is a result of the *active*, not passive, consent of the "governed". This is profound. In the tyranny of being governed by elected representatives, we do not have any opportunity to withdraw our consent. Silence is considered consent.

Silent consent is how the powers-that-not-ought-to-be, get away with their deceptions, adhesive contracts, propaganda, wars, etc. This is the problem that sociocracy solves. And it solves it in a profound way, one that corresponds exactly to our nature.

Sociocratic Organizational Structure

Sociocratic organized circles should not have less than 3 people and not more than 40 people. The number of circles can vary with the complexity of the community. Voting is never necessary. Polling only obtains a sense of the opinions of the people in a Ward, Jural Assembly, County, State, Nation, etc, but it is never binding. Everything that happens is the result of a voluntary initiative carried out by inspired individuals who form sociocratic circles to implement the aim of their circle. In a Sociocratic organized society, everything that affects the society passes through the healthy human judgment of people who know each other and work together to accomplish something they agree would be good. No circle committed to the Golden Rule ever consents to violate anyone's rights. The perception of a harm is resolved by submitting an affidavit to the Grand Jury, which is duty bound to determine genuine probable cause before issuing an indictment or presentment.

The number of circles will increase as the organization grows. Circles that become too large may split into more specific circles. Circles that are too small may merge with other circles. There is usually a General Circle that has the overall or most general responsibility for the organization. It is made up of leaders and delegates from the top level circles. Circle Organizing means that each circle is fully responsible for its domain (accomplishing its aim). Each circle's records are available to everyone so they can know anything and everything they want to know about what is going on in the organization.

The Ward or neighborhood (10 families), has a General Circle that meets occasionally. It is made up of someone from each family. The leader is likely someone who also has a role at another level. The delegate is someone the Ward General Circle chooses to represent a particular concern of theirs at the Village or Town Circle level. A Village is 10 Wards, a Town is 10 Villages, and a County is 10 Towns. Each has a General Circle made up of the leaders and delegates from more specific circles. The Village General Circle has responsibility for a specific area such as the historic district or the beach. The Town General Circle is similar to the Board of Selectmen in a New England Town, but it is made up of the leaders and delegates of the various town committees (circles) such as the 'Highway Circle', the 'Planning Circle', etc. At the County Level, the General Circle is likely to be the Administration of the Jural Assembly with sub-circles for the Court House, Vital Records, Notary (responsible for the selection of Juries and administering Due Process), Sheriff, Bank, etc. We can imagine this all developing from our Imagining Community Circle.

In our original Imagining Community Circle, each person may identify with a particular aspect of community and desire to develop that aspect further. For example, I would take on the responsibility for representing the Juno Moneta aspect of money. My wife might decide to take on responsibility for the community being prepared for disasters. The members of the Unity Team might join the Imagining Community Circle and take on convening an additional circle. Margaret might take on the responsibility to train the administrators and form an Administrator's Circle; Niki might form the Jury Education Circle, Michele might form the Facilitators Circle, or maybe the Home Schooling Circle; Darlene might create the Chaplains Circle: David might create a Rmarketplace General Circle in California and let it grow from there.

Each one of us would become the Convenor (and probably the Leader) of the new circle. Each new circle that forms would select a Delegate to represent them in the Imagining Community Circle. The circle that I convene would select a Delegate to represent it in the Imagining Community Circle in which I, as Convenor, would still participate. Now the Imagining Community Circle benefits from my commitment to Juno Moneta and the Delegate's ability to represent the work of the Juno Moneta Circle. The Leader and the Delegate both participating in a specific circle and in the more general circle assures that the communication in the developing organization is the 'glue' that holds the organization together. This is called "double linking" of circles.

The only way for everything to stay coherent and not fall into chaos is the double linking of the circles. The Juno Moneta Circle will naturally give rise to the desire of someone in that circle to take on marketing. They will form the Marketing Juno Moneta Circle, which will select a delegate to represent it in the Juno Moneta Circle. A member of the Marketing Juno Moneta Circle may desire to organize the Local Food System Circle. The Local Food System Circle would select a Delegate to the Marketing Juno Moneta Circle, which is represented in the Juno Moneta Circle, which is represented in the Imagining Community Circle.

The Imagining Community Circle might very well give rise to the Ward Republic Circle or the Jural Assembly Circle, or the Reinhabit the Republic Circle. Each of these would have double linked circles they need to accomplish their tasks. And so it goes, one voluntary initiative after another, all manifesting the vision cultivated in the Imagining Community Circle.

Training

Sociocracy is easy to grasp theoretically, but to become skilled at it, requires dedicated training. The best training that we are aware of is provided by <u>Sociocracy for All</u>. The main advantage to training with them is that one joins their community of practice and one has a ready-made sounding board for the issues that arise in implementing sociocracy.

The training is from a simple introduction through certification as a trainer. There are numerous conferences and an annual conference to stay connected with the other advocates of Sociocracy.

Once there is a willingness to learn and use sociocracy, educating ourselves about the practical funding mechanisms is the next step.

Funding Mechanisms

Common Good Payment System

There is a very well conceived and implemented payment system called Common Good. It is based on Juno, the unit of value, being the US Dollar ($), and the Moneta, the means of exchange, being Common Good (CG). The Common Good is the currency that a Common Good Community or Common Good Jural Assembly issues to implement the shift to a society that benefits everyone. In fact, the Society to Benefit Everyone, Inc., a Massachusetts not-for-profit organization, is doing business as Common Good. The Common Good Payment System is being implemented in Greenfield, MA, and the Pioneer Valley. The Unity Team has developed a slide show which describes the Common Good Payment System and is listed in the EndNotes

♥ + $ = ⓖ

The Common Good Payment system is based on an agreement to use Common Good (CG) currency instead of dollars at any vendor that accepts them. The Common Good Payment System is similar to PayPal or Venmo, or other payment systems in that it is integrated into the banking system. However, it differs from any other payment system in that we, the members, control the CG, the Moneta. Having our own Moneta independent of the US Dollar is the training ground we need to create the world we know in our hearts. It has all of the benefits of a complementary currency, namely:

- it is honest and transparent,
- it is based on cooperation and collaboration (rather than competition),
- it is an agreement,
- it is issued without any costs nor interest, and
- it benefits the community.

It has none of the drawbacks of a complementary currency, because it is connected to and works parallel to the existing monetary system. It has the ability to switch CG back to the existing monetary system for access to the broader marketplace. Common Good is a 501(c)(3) nonprofit registered as a money services business (MSB) which issues forms 1099-K as required by the IRS, but it is nonetheless an autonomous community-supported system with the ability of a community to establish its own administration.

When one signs up for Common Good, one transfers money (US dollars) from one's bank account to the Common Good Escrow Bank Account. The system creates a CG account for the new member and issues into it - with an accounting entry in its database - the same amount of CG (Moneta) as dollars one had transferred. There are now both dollars and CG in the Common Good Payment System, so we just doubled the money supply with our agreement to use CG instead of dollars. One spends one's CG with either one's Common Good card, or a picture of that card on one's phone running the CGPay App. The vendor uses a smartphone to take a picture of the QR code on one's phone and the system debits one's CG account and credits the vendor's account.

The dollars in the Common Good Escrow account are available for transferring dollars back to one's bank account, thereby extinguishing the CG. As long as there are more dollars going into the Escrow Account than coming out, the pool of dollars will grow. When we have enough experience to know that the members have taken responsibility for the system and it is working well, we will be able to decide how much CG to issue to fund the projects we determine are worthwhile. The Common Good website has more information and a video that goes into more detail.

To implement Common Good, we need a circle capable of managing the open source software and the administration of the payment system. We also need a circle of people willing to promote it and enroll businesses together with their customers and their suppliers. To get the full benefit of Common Good, we need to create economic circles, so that our Moneta may circulate, rather than being converted back to dollars.

To derive the most benefit from the Common Good system, my recommendation is to use it to invest in local businesses, especially worker-owned and multi stakeholder cooperatives.

Local Investing

The Official Story says investing is risky and normal people must be protected so that they only invest in approved investment vehicles managed by experts. This means that publicly traded companies have a huge advantage when it comes to raising capital. They can buy up the small, profitable companies that are providing goods and services to their local town or region. Those profits are siphoned off to the mega-rich and no longer contribute to local prosperity. Local businesses usually only have access to retained earnings, family capital, or bank loans. This is what the local investing movement is inspired to remedy. Investing in local businesses has huge benefits for the communities they serve. The return on investment is not just interest or a dividend, but a prospering, vibrant community with a rich culture and appreciation for the commons and the common good. Local investors consistently say they are motivated to invest in the people, not just the business idea, and for the benefit to their community.

Creating local investing groups or participating in established ones can be a powerful tool in creating the new model. There is much to learn about the Slow Money movement to bring money down to earth and invest in local farming and food systems, the Local Investment Opportunities Network (LION) and Michael Shuman's The Mainstreet Journal, are additional resources to consider.

When we need money for one of our projects, it is always possible to launch a crowdfunding campaign to get the seed money needed. Check out what even very ambitious projects are doing, such as Solar Roadways.

Cooperatives and Open Book Management

Cooperatives

The <u>Cooperative Movement</u> has always offered an alternative to the official story about what a business should be. Consumer cooperatives bring the values of the consumer members into a retail business and share the profits. The worker-cooperative form is a powerful way to overcome the Capital vs the Labor divide. Producer coops give the smaller businesses in an industry the marketing clout they need to compete. The multi stakeholder cooperative holds the most promise for harmonizing the so-called competing interests of investors, producers, workers, and consumers. The <u>Cooperative Development Institute</u> in Shelburne Falls, MA is among the best of the Coops that promote Cooperative Ownership. The International Cooperative Alliance (ICA) is a good source of information about Cooperatives and their website is very useful.

It used to be that <u>Credit Unions</u> were credit cooperatives among affiliated members before they were regulated into becoming just like banks. Credit Unions are still preferable for retail banking because they are more locally oriented and safer than the Too Big to Fail (TBTF) banks. The TBTF banks will surely get in trouble again, but they will be "<u>bailed in</u>" by their creditors and depositors, not bailed out by the government, which places undue burden on taxpayers. Financial reforms under the Dodd-Frank Act eliminated bailouts and opened the door for bail-ins. Bail-ins allow banks to convert debt into equity to increase their capital requirements. The Common Good Payment System is a better way to access our community credit than Credit Unions.

Cooperatives are an important way to create distributive justice because they are organized to give the people a say in their vision, mission, and operations, and the profits are distributed *equitably* (according to merit) and not equally.

Many of us are familiar with and maybe even belong to a Natural Food Store Consumer Coop and are familiar with the integrity of the products stocked. Worker-owned coops are usually not so visible. Two that I am familiar with in Greenfield, MA, are Real Pickles and PV². They both participate in Common Good and their products have real integrity. Producer Coops, such as Florida's Natural Orange Juice and Organic Valley, give their farmer/owners national distribution, and Ace Hardware gives its retail owners the benefits of national scale to compete with the likes of Walmart or Lowes.

In the United States, cooperatives are an increasing part of our lives. Consider the following statistics from the IDWC:

- 29,000 cooperatives operate in every sector of the U.S. economy.
- 1 billion people are members of cooperatives worldwide.
- 1 in 3 Americans are co-op members holding 350 million co-op memberships worldwide.
- U.S. cooperatives generate 2 million jobs each year, contribute $652 billion in annual sales, and possess $3 trillion in assets.
- 92 million Americans turn to 7,500 credit unions – which are cooperatives – for their financial services.
- Most of the America's 2 million farmers are farmer co-op members providing 250,000 jobs and $8 billion in annual wages.
- 1.2 million U.S. families of all income levels live in homes owned and operated through cooperatives.
- 42 million Americans rely on electricity from 900 rural electric co-ops in 47 states – making up 42% of the nation's electric distribution and covering 75% of our land mass.
- 233 million people are served by co-op-owned and affiliated insurance companies.
- 1.2 million rural Americans are served by 260 telephone cooperatives in 31 states.
- 50,000 U.S. families rely on cooperative daycare facilities and preschools for the care of their children.

The defining characteristic of a cooperative is member ownership and the right to share in the profits and to have some say in the governance.

There are seven voluntary, <u>universal co-operative principles</u>. Each of which contrasts with capitalist firms:

1. "Voluntary and Open Membership" (in contrast to coerced/involuntary participation)
2. "Democratic Member Control" (in contrast to nondemocratic control)
3. "Member Economic Participation" (in contrast to purely transactional relationships and closed-book management)
4. "Autonomy and Independence" (in contrast to state-owned or corporate ownership)
5. "Education, Training, and Information" (in contrast to "<u>mushroom management</u>" where workers are "kept in the dark," and information is intentionally funneled through power channels)
6. "Cooperation among Cooperatives" (in contrast to competition amongst firms)
7. "Concern for Community" (in contrast to purely product or profit-oriented concerns)

As we develop a real Juno Moneta Monetary System, we will realize the full potential of the Cooperative Movement to become the society that benefits everyone.

Open Book Management

Cooperatives are the ideal organizational form for sociocratic governance to take root. The circle, led by its aim and whose members' job is the aim, has the autonomy to decide how to accomplish its aim. This speaks to the innate desire for autonomy and purpose, and continuous improvement. The true power of the sociocratic and cooperative form is still to be realized, but a start has been made with <u>Open Book Management</u>. The premise of Open Book Management is that since the success of the enterprise depends on the intelligent work of the members, they will be able to work more intelligently and effectively when they understand how what they do contributes to the bottom line. The members need to understand the Income Statement, the Balance Sheet, and the Statement of Cash Flows for their company, their department, and their circle. When the people understand the finances as well as they understand the work they do, they will be able to participate much more effectively in the success of the enterprise. Open book companies establish their budget and goals for the coming year or years based on the commitment of the members to move a critical number in a positive direction. An example is the effect of choosing to reduce or even eliminate, warranty claims and returns of defective products. Nearly everyone in the company can contribute to that goal. The increase in profitability can be substantial and could be celebrated with the whole company going on a cruise together.

<u>National Center for Employee Ownership</u> did a study comparing 54 companies that practiced Open-Book Management with 54 very similar companies that did not and found a significant advantage in the Open-Book Companies.

The Jural Assembly

This book aims to inspire the creation of Jural Assembly Communities in every county in the country. A Jural Assembly Community has a **Culture** based on **Freedom**, a **Society** based on **Justice,** and an **Economy** based on voluntary **Community**,

Using the ideas described in this book, we may create a thriving community by sharing with each other in concrete terms our imagination of the ideals of individual Freedom, social Justice, and collaborative Community, and our intention for manifesting them.

Here are some concrete ideas to share regarding Freedom, Justice and Community:

1. People, who are supported and thus *free* to pursue the transcendent purpose they choose to dedicate their life to accomplishing, will become self-aware and will create a Culture based on:

   a. Science - the quest for Truth;
   b. Art - the desire for Beauty; and
   c. Spirituality/Religion/Education - the inspiration to do the Good.

2. Self-aware individuals will form a Society that provides the functions of governance to each other out of the sense of *justice* that dwells in our hearts, namely "We do unto others as we would have others do unto us", and we "Do No Harm".

   a. By inspiring rather than coercing;
   b. By respecting everyone's right to the capital their capacities warrant.
   c. By participating in adjudicating harm and showing up when called to serve on a Jury.
   d. By paying attention and actively consenting to proposals in the circles in which we participate.

3. Self-aware individuals will create a *community* and sustainable Economy by collaborating with each other to provide everything that we need and desire.

   a. By taking responsibility to provide what we are interested in and capable of providing.
   b. By volunteering to work in other related projects.
   c. By participating in the various circles we feel are necessary to express needs and desires and assure they are being met.

The End Notes contains a link to the Just Abundance website of a list of people (and their websites) who I call <u>Wayshowers and Truth Tellers</u>. These people are seeking the truth and can show the way forward. Each of them is advocating that the future lies in the security of a community in which we are pledged to mutual support. These are the guides and their followers we will need to enroll in our ideas about the Jural Assembly as the way forward.

Additionally, there are <u>sample bylaws</u> for a Jural Assembly and a <u>Consent-based Self-Governance Handbook</u> accessible from the End Notes.

As the ideas of the Jural Assembly are gradually transformed from mere ideas to motivating ideals and practices, we may expect that our confidence will grow as we feel genuinely supported in being free and becoming ever more integrated - sovereign. We may expect that a great love for our potential and for our fellow man, our neighbors, will well up in us and become the powerful moral compass for our lives.

Conclusion

The life-empowering, fear-conquering ideas that we need in order to come together to create the world that we know in our hearts, are available. They reside in each of us and many of them are enumerated here. When we gather to share what is in our hearts, share with each other what Freedom means to us, what Justice means to us, and what Community means to us, we will be in the process of creating the new world.

Ring the Bell of Freedom, Ring the Bell of Justice, Ring the Bell of Community, and enjoy the warmth of the love that arises out of simple, genuine interest in each other's struggles and triumphs. Let us share our hopes and fears and let us embrace the better angels of our nature.

Endnotes

See Just Abundance website for additional information on these topics

- For EndNotes: https://www.justabundance.org/fj
- Appendixes: https://www.justabundance.org/appendixes

Sociocracy

- https://en.wikipedia.org/wiki/Sociocracy
- https://www.sociocracyforall.org/sociocracy/
- Ted Rau, *Many Voices One Song* and *Collective Power.*
- https://www.ic.org/community-bookstore/product/many-voices-one-song/
- Just Abundance link to a very worthwhile introduction to Sociocracy similar to a slide show. https://www.justabundance.org/appendix-5
- Intentional Communities website: https://IC.org

Group Size

https://www.sociocracy.info/maximum-size-for-rounds/

Common Good

- https://CommonGood.earth.
- http://www.nonprofitfacts.com/MA/Society-To-Benefit-Everyone-Inc-Common-Good-Finance.html
- https://www.guidestar.org/profile/20-5280780
- The slide show from the Unity Team Seminar https://www.justabundance.org/appendix-5
- Video: https://www.youtube.com/watch?v=LCbO1WNGk74

Buy Up The Small, Profitable Companies

https://deeprootsathome.com/popular-small-health-food-companies-sold-out/

Slow Money

https://slowmoney.org/

Local Investment Opportunity Network

https://en.wikipedia.org/wiki/Local_Investing_Opportunity_Network

The Mainstreet Journal,

https://www.themainstreetjournal.org/about-us

Crowdfunding

10 best crowdfund ing platforms
https://www.shopify.com/blog/crowdfunding-sites#

1. Best overall: Kickstarter
2. Runner-up: Indiegogo
3. Best for small businesses: Fundable
4. Best for Shopify stores: Crowdfunder
5. Best for content creators: Patreon
6. Best for UK and Europe: Crowdcube
7. Best for personal fundraising: GoFundMe
8. Best for nonprofits: Mightycause
9. Best for real estate crowdfunding: CrowdStreet
10. Best for high-growth startups: StartEngine

Solar Roadways

- https://solarroadways.com/
- https://www.startengine.com/offering/solar-roadways

Cooperative Movement

- https://en.wikipedia.org/wiki/History_of_the_cooperative_movement
- https://ica.coop/en/history-co-operative-movement
- https://www.encyclopedia.com/social-sciences-and-law/sociology-and-social-reform/social-reform/cooperative-movement
- https://en.wikipedia.org/wiki/Worker_cooperative

Cooperative Development Institute

- Website: www.cdi.coop
- Their Guide to Establishing a Cooperative: https://cdi.coop/wp-content/uploads/2015/03/start-up-packet-2015-web.pdf

International Cooperative Alliance (ICA)

https://ica.coop/

Credit Unions

https://en.wikipedia.org/wiki/Credit_unions_in_the_United_States

Bail In

https://www.investopedia.com/terms/b/bailin.asp

IWDC

Independent Welding Distributors Cooperative

https://www.iwdc.coop/why-a-coop/facts-about-cooperatives-1

Universal Co-Operative Principles

- https://www.iatp.org/sites/default/files/Seven_Principles_of_Cooperatives_The.pdf
- https://www.acca.coop/co-op-principles

Mushroom Management

https://en.wikipedia.org/wiki/Mushroom_management

Open Book Management

- https://en.wikipedia.org/wiki/Open-book_management
- https://en.wikipedia.org/wiki/Open-book_management
- https://www.youtube.com/watch?v=WdrXDfNPa-E&list=PLTXjlXwe8oegU-HFLdH8L8GEQAm_0TWgH

National Center for Employee Ownership

- https://www.nceo.org/articles/open-book-management
- https://www.nceo.org/ownership-culture

Wayshowers and Truth Tellers

https://www.justabundance.org/appendix-5

Sample Bylaws

https://www.justabundance.org/appendix-5

Consent-based Self-Governance Handbook

https://www.justabundance.org/appendix-5

ABOUT THE AUTHOR

I come from an Anthroposophical family, attended 13 years of Waldorf School in New York City, dropped out of Bowdoin College and graduated from the Camphill Seminar (for special education and social therapy) I am a member of the Anthroposophical Society and The School of Spiritual Science and its Social Science Section. I have been living and worked in intentional communities oriented to manifesting Rudolf Steiner's spiritual science most of my life.

My career has been creating community with people with mental disabilities in an intentional community called the Cadmus Lifesharing Association in which everyone is a volunteer. I wish I had known Sociocracy during that time because consensus is a lousy way to govern an intentional community. The motto of the Cadmus Lifesharing Association is "Everyone is perfect in their essential being and everyone is handicapped in bringing that essence to expression". In Cadmus, we recognize and further each other's abilities and we recognize and compensate for each other's disabilities. This experience is what gives me confidence that we can extend this to our neighborhoods and Wards.

In 2012 I retired and shifted my volunteer efforts to monetary reform and read just about every book there is about the nature of money. I have participated in numerous efforts to revendicate the promise of the Declaration of Independence. When I was expelled from a group working to reinhabit the Republic a small group of us formed what we call the Unity Team to come up with the ideas we need to succeed in uniting the freedom movement. This book is a fruit of my transcendent purpose to create sovereign communities based on our common sense, sense of justice and the primary tool that the sovereign uses to create the conditions in which, we the people, live, which is money creation. A community or ward that, issues the money to accomplish the things that we agree would be good and regulates the money supply so that it is always properly measuring the value of the goods and services we make available to each other will create a society that benefits everyone.

Creating Common Good Communities governed Sociocratically as described in Chapter 5 is what I expect this book will help me do. I aim to help create a new civilization that respects our essential being and heals our planet. The principle of self-actualization will become the principle of civilization.

Printed in the United States
by Baker & Taylor Publisher Services